THE **WHARNCLIFFE C**

WAKEFIELD & DISTRICT

VE Celebrations at Fryston

Wakefield Cultural Services, Jack Hulme Collection

THE **WHARNCLIFFE COMPANION** TO

WAKEFIELD & DISTRICT

AN **A** TO **Z** OF LOCAL HISTORY

LEN MARKHAM

Colonel John Morris

Wharncliffe Books

This book is dedicated to the inspirational memory of Colonel John Morris of South Elmsall, a patriot who never gave up the Royalist cause in Yorkshire and who died for his friend.

First published in Great Britain in 2005 by
Wharncliffe Books
an imprint of
Pen & Sword Books Ltd
47 Church Street
Barnsley
South Yorkshire
S70 2AS

ISBN 1-903425-89-1

A CIP catalogue record for this book is
available from the British Library

Typeset in 10/11.5pt Plantin by Wharncliffe Books
Printed and bound in England by CPI UK

Pen & Sword Books Ltd incorporates the Imprints of Pen & Sword Aviation,
Pen & Sword Maritime, Pen & Sword Military, Wharncliffe Books,
Pen & Sword Select, Pen and Sword Military Classics and Leo Cooper.

For a complete list of Wharncliffe titles, please contact
Wharncliffe Books Limited
47 Church Street, Barnsley, South Yorkshire, S70 2AS, England
E-mail: enquiries@pen-and-sword.co.uk
Website: www.wharncliffebooks.co.uk

Contents

Foreword

The Wakefield district has a rich history and heritage, ranging from Castleford's Roman origins through Pontefract Castle civil war battles to Wakefield's important role in the Industrial Revolution with some of the oldest mines in the country. This book will take you through some of the events and to some of the places which make the District what is it today.

We celebrate our heritage and our past in how we plan for the future. We will enjoy the work of two world-famous sculptors both born in the District - Barbara Hepworth and Henry Moore - in wonderful new buildings planned for Wakefield and Castleford.

Councillor Peter Box, Leader, City of Wakefield Metropolitan District Council

The Hepworth - a world-class art gallery on the waterfront in Wakefield - and the Castleford Forum - a heritage centre - will be architectural landmarks, standing among others we are already proud of, like Wakefield Cathedral, the Chantry Chapel, the Theatre Royal and Opera House and grand town houses of St John's Square.

The unique National Mining Museum takes visitors 140 metres underground to see what life was really like at the coalface from the sight of a child at work to modern production methods.

Wakefield and Pontefract Museum both tell fascinating stories from our past – eccentric Victorian explorer Charles Waterton who came back from South America with a collection of strange animals preserved for future generations and the liquorice industry in Pontefract dating back to medieval times.

We have iron-age settlements at South Kirkby, Roman remains at Castleford, one of the oldest remaining coaching houses at Wentbridge - a haunt of highwaymen. We have close links with the legend of Robin Hood and a village which was cut off by the plague.

We are proud of our history and heritage. I hope this book will help you understand and appreciate what has influenced our growth and development over the centuries, making Wakefield and district what it is today.

Peter Box, Leader, City of Wakefield MDC

Introduction

The WHARNCLIFFE COMPANION TO WAKEFIELD & DISTRICT is the first book of its kind, presenting together, a concise history and gazetteer of Wakefield and its Metropolitan District in one easy-to-use A-Z format. It combines signpost information about modern facilities for investment, business and leisure together with a wealth of interesting and intriguing historical details about all aspects of the city and its district.

The genesis of the book has been a long one, the author, who worked in central and local government in Wakefield for over twenty years, finding a sparsity of comprehensive information that encapsulated the dynamism of the modern district together with the long history of the area in one readable volume. The aim therefore has been to rectify this omission by creating an amalgam, combining the best elements of an encyclopaedia and a pocket guidebook to create one volume, suitable for visitors, residents and the business community alike.

It has been a stimulating exercise for the author. What has jumped out of the pages with the passion of a hundred front-row forwards has been the sheer scale and diversity of the district's achievement in all spheres of human endeavour. Wakefield and its citizens have truly made a benevolent mark on the modern world, this little book, perhaps for the very first time, showing the astonishing range of that achievement.

The WHARNCLIFFE COMPANION TO WAKEFIELD & DISTRICT has over 500 entries. Many of these are subject-connected, the use of emboldened type indicating such cross-references.

Any ambitious undertaking of this nature, risks errors and omissions but the project is an ongoing one that can, with reader contributions, be corrected, enlarged and enriched in subsequent editions. Any updated or new information about the ongoing development and history of Wakefield will be gratefully received and used in subsequent publications.

Acknowledgments

In compiling this companion, and attempting to capture the essential essence and character of Wakefield and its district, I have consulted widely and examined hundreds of books, leaflets, pamphlets, reports, contracts, letters, obituaries and internet entries, supplementing my researches with personal memories and interviews with old colleagues, academics, employers, workers, librarians and the curators of museums. The entire exercise has been a compelling and an ever-surprising experience that has revealed a rich seam of human endeavour and achievement that has enriched the nation. Wakefieldians - and if such a word does not exist, well it ought to – should be proud!

I have been assisted all the way by a fine body of men, my especial thanks going to John Goodchild of the John Goodchild Collection, Richard Van Riel of Pontefract Museum, my good friend and amazing bibliophile Rodger Matthews who was formerly the district's Chief Environmental Services Officer and who steered me in many fruitful directions and the Leader of Wakefield Metropolitan District Council, Councillor Peter Box who has encouraged this project from the start.

Len Markham, Ratton Manor, Eastbourne, 2005.

The Merrie City

Wakefield – a rugged, no-nonsense, poke-you-in-the eye-with-a-stuffed-whippet, waste nothing, 'mine's a pint and make sure you fill it t'line lad', sort of town. Unsophisticated it isn't but what it lacks in fancy airs and graces it more than makes up in a capacity for work, invention and bold endeavour that has, in its long history, brought prosperity, fame and fortune and a reputation for enjoying itself.

A large market town renowned for its 'course drapery' in the early sixteenth century, Wakefield became the centre of the clothing trade before the ascendancy of Leeds and Bradford, coal mining underpinning the local economy and transforming the physical and social landscape of the area for generations until the demise of the industry in the latter half of the twentieth century. Pit closures brought hardship on a massive scale but in the new millennium, Wakefield has taken advantage of its arterially advantageous position in the nation's road and rail networks to forge a bright future, new, strategically placed industrial, commercial and business parks energising the economy alongside flagship retail and sporting developments connected by major motorways.

Much of the legacy of industrialisation – pit heads, spoil heaps and processing plants - has gone and the countryside has been reclaimed, creating a surprisingly rural setting for the many former mining towns and villages that have been modernised taking advantage of UK government and European grants. In just two generations, the local workforce has exchanged its miner's lamp for its lap top computer and although the smut and grime may have disappeared, not so the enterprising spirit, the camaraderie, the burning individuality and the collective energy that still epitomises – particularly in scrums and tackles – the ebullient and effusively friendly people of Wakefield. This little book is dedicated to them and one Wakefield district man in particular whose memory makes you proud to be a Tyke.

Useful Addresses

WAKEFIELD DISTRICT
INVESTMENT/EMPLOYMENT/TRAINING OPPORTUNITIES

WAKEFIELD FIRST
(The Development Agency for the Wakefield District)
PO Box 159, Newton Bar, Leeds Road, Wakefield, WF1 1ZD. Telephone 01924 306313 –
email: first@wakefield.gov.uk; website www.firstwakefield.com
(This agency should be the first point of contact for all enquiries about business, commercial,
training, skills and investment opportunities offering relevant socio-economic data and full
details of industrial estates and business parks and major residential developments)

CASTLEFORD WOMEN'S CENTRE
1 York Street, Castleford, WF10 1 JS. Telephone 01977 511581

FIVE TOWNS RESOURCE AND TECHNOLOGY CENTRE
Welbeck Street, Castleford, WF10 1DR. Telephone 01977 723940/723948

MINSTHORPE COMMUNITY COLLEGE
Minsthorpe Lane, South Elmsall, Pontefract, WF9 2UJ.
Telephone 01977 723810. Website www.minsthorpe.wakefield.sch.uk

WAKEFIELD COLLEGE
Telephone 01924 789115
www.servtobusiness.co.uk

WESTFIELD RESOURCE AND ENTERPRISE CENTRE
Westfield Lane, South Elmsall, WF9 2PY. Telephone 01997 645141.

WAKEFIELD DISTRICT
HISTORICAL, LEISURE AND RESEARCH ATTRACTIONS

CASTLEFORD TIGERS RUGBY LEAGUE FOOTBALL CLUB
The Jungle, Wheldon Road, Castleford. Telephone 01977 552674 Website: www.castiger.com

CLARKE HALL
Aberford Road, Wakefield.
Telephone 01924 302703/302700.
Website: www.clarke-hall.co.uk

FEATHERSTONE ROVERS RUGBY LEAGUE FOOTBALL CLUB
Lionheart Stadium, Post Office Road, Featherstone, WF7 5EN.
Telephone 01977 602723.

FREEPORT, CASTLEFORD
Telephone 01977 520153
Website: www.freeportcastleford.com

THE JOHN GOODCHILD COLLECTION
Local History Study Centre, Below Central Library, Drury Lane, Wakefield, WF1 2TD.
Telephone 01924 298929.

HEMSWORTH WATER PARK
Hoyle Mill Road, Kinsley, Pontefract. Telephone 01977 617617.

HERONRY AND WATERTON COUNTRYSIDE DISCOVERY CENTRE
Anglers Country Park, Haw Park Lane, Wintersett, Wakefield, WF4 2EB.
Telephone 01924 303980

KINSLEY GREYHOUND STADIUM
96 Wakefield Road, Kinsley, Pontefract,
WF9 5EH. Telephone 01977 610946
Website:www.kinsleydogs.co.uk

NATIONAL COAL MINING MUSEUM FOR ENGLAND
Caphouse Colliery, New Road, Overton, Wakefield, WF4 4RH.
Telephone 01924 848806.
Website: www.ncm.org.uk

PONTEFRACT RACECOURSE
Pontefract Park, Pontefract
Telephone 01977 703224
Website: www.pontefract-races.co.uk

PUGNEYS COUNTRY PARK
Asdale Road, Wakefield, WF2 7EQ. Telephone 01924 302360.

WAKEFIELD ART GALLERY
Wentworth Terrace, Wakefield, WF1 2HQ. Telephone 01924 305796.

WAKEFIELD-EMLEY AFC
Belle Vue, Doncaster Road, Wakefield, WF1 5HT. Telephone 01924 216111/848398.

WAKEFIELD MUSEUM
Wood Street, Wakefield, WF1 2HQ. Telephone 01924 305356.

WAKEFIELD THEATRE ROYAL
Drury Lane, Wakefield, WF1 2TE. Telephone 01924 211311.

WAKEFIELD TRINITY WILDCATS RUGBY LEAGUE FOOTBALL CLUB
Doncaster Road, Belle Vue, Wakefield, WF1 5HT. Telephone 01924 211611.
Website:www.wildcatsrl.com

WEST YORKSHIRE ARCHIVE SERVICE
Wakefield Headquarters, Registry of Deeds, Newstead Road, Wakefield, WF1 2DE.
Telephone 01924 305980.

XSCAPE
Colorado Way, Glasshoughton, Castleford, WF10 4TA
Telephone 01977 523000
Website:www.xscape.co.uk

YORKSHIRE ART CIRCUS
School Lane, Glasshoughton, Castleford, WF10 4QH. Telephone 01977 550401

YORKSHIRE SCULPTURE PARK
West Bretton, Wakefield, WF4 4LG.
Telephone 01924 830302
Website:www.ysp.co.uk

The Wharncliffe Companion to Wakefield & District

A

ACKWORTH, HIGH, LOW AND MOOR TOP

Three neighbouring villages, the latter larger settlement abutting Fitzwilliam and its former colliery. Ackworth was one of the resting places for the body of St Cuthbert who died in 688, loyal monks relocating the corpse to escape the attentions of the marauding Danes. The local church is named after him and there is an effigy of the saint inside. Ackworth has a wilful and independent past. In 1488, outraged villagers refused to pay taxes levied to support the war in France but were defeated in an armed conflict with the Crown. The area suffered badly in successive plagues, the **PLAGUE STONE** surviving to this day. Ackworth Old Hall was erected as a manor house in the early 1600s. It was once owned by James I who sold it in 1628 for £384. The ghost of hanged highwayman William **NEVISON**, who used a hideout above the doorway to escape capture, still haunts the hall.

Seventeenth century High Ackworth. Extract from *Old Yorkshire* edited by William Smith, 1884.

Ackworth School from the Great Garden. Extract from Old Yorkshire *edited by William Smith, 1884.*

ACKWORTH SCHOOL

A celebrated academy founded by Dr John **FOTHERGILL**. It was originally established by Thomas **CORAM** as a foundling hospital for the 'maintenance and education of exposed and deserted young children.' The establishment became a **QUAKERS** school in 1779. Five hundred pupils were eventually recruited from all over England, some embarking on apprenticeships with local tradesmen, others successfully entering the worlds of academia, politics and business. The impressive school buildings have, as their nucleus, a thirteen-bayed, two-storied, pedimented centre block - colonnades, courtyards and Tuscan columns in the adjacent structures creating a classical ambience for learning still infused with a religious ethos. A Meeting House was added in similar style in 1847. Opposite the school entrance is an interesting stone signpost dated 1805. There is a second such post nearby.

ADAM AND LOW

Two rival preachers were competing for a lectureship by delivering sermons to the same congregation who would decide the contest. Mr Low preached on the Bible text 'Adam, where art thou?' Mr Adam, a clever wit who had been educated in Wakefield, went to the pulpit next and began by introducing the subject of his homily, using the Bible passage immediately following that of his rival, saying 'Lo, here am I.' He got the job.

AIR RAIDS

Wakefield was first targeted by the Luftwaffe on 28 August 1940, bombs, falling on Norton Street, Belle Vue, injuring four people and destroying six houses. In December 1940, a cluster of bombs fell on the city before the air raid sounded. One 1000-kilogram device fell on Chantry Road Lupset but it failed to explode, leaving a crater 14 feet across and 8 feet deep. It was a tense Christmas. The bomb was only defused in February. The worst attack came on the night of 14 March 1941, two bombs hitting Thornes Road, killing six residents and injuring four more. Explosions damaged or destroyed scores of houses, local ARP crews dousing the flames with water pumped from the **CALDER RIVER** in a show of preparedness. An unexploded bomb fell on Lord Mayor's Walk in **PONTEFRACT** on 8 August 1942.

AIRE, RIVER

Rising in Malham, West Yorkshire's principal commercial waterway flows through Leeds. Joined by the **CALDER RIVER** at **CASTLEFORD** it continues eastward to **KNOTTINGLEY** – where it is connected to the **KNOTTINGLEY AND GOOLE CANAL** – and its confluence with the Ouse River at Airmyn.

AIRE AND CALDER NAVIGATION

Inland waterway utilising the **AIRE RIVER** and the **CALDER RIVER**. The necessary improvements – clearances, enlargements, course straightening, the construction of cuts, locks and towing paths – and the imposition of tolls, were approved by Act of Parliament in 1699, providing navigation from Weeland to Leeds and Wakefield. For many years, coal transportation was the lifeblood of operations. Sailing boats were originally employed in the lower tidal reaches of the waterway. Tugs and horses were used further inland.

ALDRED, EBENEZER

Regarded as the promoter of Wakefield's first modern mill, this somewhat eccentric gentleman, who later became a church minister, set up a factory in 1783 to manufacture cloth on land adjoining Westgate Common, an early steam engine powering its water wheel. The enterprise was not commercially successful and he eventually withdrew to the High Peak of Derbyshire to follow a religious calling. His callings were loud and he went to London, claiming to be a prophet and calling out from a boat on the Thames that London was doomed. He was the author of *The Little Book*.

Allinson's Flour Mill from the River Aire. The river is now cleaner! LMA

ALLINSON
Brand name of stone ground flour produced at Queens Mill, **CASTLEFORD**.

ALLINSON, THOMAS RICHARD
Pioneering doctor born near Manchester in 1858. Early in his career, he discovered Naturopathy, a medical regime that avoids the use of drugs and advocates a diet of natural unprocessed foods. A vegetarian non-smoker who was one of the first in his field to recognise the dangers of smoking, he was heavily criticised for his views and was struck off the medical register. Undaunted, he continued to stress the importance of a healthy diet and he championed the use of wholemeal grain, criticising the production of mechanical roller milled flour favoured by the masses. Eventually, his wisdom was acknowledged and he was offered reinstatement to the medical profession. In typical bullish fashion, he refused and continued to style himself doctor, adding the initials Ex-LRRP.Ed (ex-Licentiate of the Royal College of Physicians and Surgeons of Edinburgh) to his name. In 1892, he bought a stone grinding flour mill in London and after his death in 1918, his company purchased similar mills in Newport, Monmouthshire and **CASTLEFORD**. The town's Queens Mill, built in 1898 on a site occupied by mills since 1122, still flourishes, its expansion in 1980 giving it twenty pairs of hand dressed French Burr stones making it the largest stone-grinding flour mill in the world.

Thomas Richard Allinson.
ADM Milling Limited

ALTOFTS
Ancient, pre-Domesday village on the south side of the **CALDER RIVER**, originally known as 'Tofts' – the homestead. It was the birthplace in 1535 of the famous explorer Martin **FROBISHER** whose home – Frobisher Hall – was demolished in 1859. Post Industrial Revolution farming gave way to mining, the settlement known as 'The Buildings' and the Pope and Pearson

pit dominating the town. In 1886, an explosion killed twenty-two men at the Silkstone Pit, the tragedy encouraging later experimental work by the mining pioneer Sir William Edward **GARFORTH**. The last shift at the colliery was on 7 October 1966. Despite local opposition, the majority of the properties comprising 'The Buildings' were demolished in the 1970s.

ALVERTHORPE

Now a suburb of Wakefield, this former independent village was, for 150 years, famous for producing high quality worsted cloth and green snooker table baize at its prominent Colbeck's Mill. Its magnificent seventeenth century hall was demolished after the Second World War. A memorial pillar with seven trees commemorates the death of seven miners who were drowned in the **LOFTHOUSE PIT DISASTER** as they worked under the village in 1973.

ALVERTHORPE HALL

This impressive mansion was demolished at the end of the Second World War. It was once the home of Henry **CLARKSON**, becoming a private school for boarders around 1855. During the eighteenth century, it had a sinister reputation as the lair of a 'boggart' or 'padfoot', a weird Lord of the Rings type creature described as having a cringing body, the size of a calf, with wild glaring eyes and vicious claws. It would rise from a nearby well dragging heavy chains and would devour the halls' servants. The hall may have been designed by Theophilus **SHELTON**.

ALVERTHORPE MEADOWS AND WRENTHORPE PARK

A once forested green oasis amidst the residential suburbs of northwest Wakefield, managed as an open access wildlife reserve and countryside recreational area for pedestrians and cyclists.

ARDSLEY, EAST AND WEST

Former colliery villages with blast furnaces. One of East Ardsley's most colourful sons was James **NAYLER**. Lee Gap Fair, established at West Ardsley about 1100 is regarded as the oldest in the country. At one time it was the most important trade fair in Europe. Such was its reputation, that it was honoured with a specially composed anthem.

ARMITAGE, REGINALD MOXON

Popular lyricist and composer whose tuneful compositions *The Sun Has Got His Hat On*, *I'm Leaning On A Lamp Post* and *Run Rabbit Run* are embedded in British wartime culture. Known by his theatre bill name - Noel Gay – he studied music at **WAKEFIELD QUEEN ELIZABETH'S GRAMMAR**

SCHOOL, the Royal College of Music and Cambridge University. He was one of the most successful British song writers of the period with a wide repertoire of compositions for dance bands, military bands, orchestras, films and musical comedies. His greatest hits, in the show *Me And My Girl* which ran in London for 1500 performances in 1937, were a song with the same title and *The Lambeth Walk* sung by the legendary Lupino Lane.

ARNATT AND ASHLEY
In 1886, the **FERRYBRIDGE** postmaster Josiah Arnatt and H M Ashley, the manager of the local iron foundry, were jointly responsible for creating a machine that successfully made the world's first automatically produced glass bottle. A reconstruction of their machine is in the Science Museum in London.

ASPDIN, JOSEPH
The founder of the Portland Cement Company who lived in **WAKEFIELD ST JOHN'S SQUARE**. Born in 1778, the eldest son of a bricklayer, he became interested in increasing the strength of bonded brickwork and carried out experiments, burning ground limestone and clay together to produce a new building material patented on 21 October 1824. The name Portland was used in reference to the materials resemblance, when set, to Portland limestone found on the Isle of Portland in Dorset, the word 'cement' deriving from the Latin term *caementum* meaning 'clipped stone'. The cement was manufactured in Kirkgate, Wakefield on the site of **WAKEFIELD PARK HILL GARDENS**, currently occupied by **WAKEFIELD KIRKGATE RAILWAY STATION**. Aspdin's works were displaced by the railway to a new site in Ings Road. The cement was used locally in the construction of the *Wakefield Arms*, nationally in housing schemes in Staffordshire and Surrey and internationally in great civil engineering projects such as the construction of the Boulder Dam project in the United States. Its inventor kept his formula a closely guarded secret. Not even his workers were privy to its secret mix. He began a promotional campaign to persuade builders to use his new material but he initially had little success. An endorsement from an impeccable source, however, changed opinions overnight. Aspdin's son, who had established a cement works of his own in London, intervened when a tunnel being dug under the Thames by Marc Isambard Brunel collapsed. Site engineer, the legendary Isambard Kingdom Brunel, used the cement to seal the breach enabling the tunnel to be pumped dry. The reputation of Portland cement was made. Aspdin, who died in 1855, is commemorated in a memorial in his local St John's Church and by gates, erected in 1938 at the eastern end of the churchyard. Lord Wolmer of the Cement and Concrete Association described Aspdin's invention as 'a product of incalculable benefit to mankind.'

B

BABY IN THE WELL

A shocking discovery was made during the routine maintenance of a well adjacent to the empty Hawthorn House in Pinfold Lane, Sandal in June 1880. Local bricklayer James Brewin pumped out the well and went to investigate the cause of a nauseating smell, descending a ladder to find the putrefied remains of a small child. The pitiful corpse was taken away in a wheelbarrow to the *Castle Inn*. The police and a surgeon were summoned and a telegram was sent to the absent tenant Mrs Ann Westmorland. A subsequent inquest failed to establish how the unfortunate baby had died or indeed if it had ever lived although the **WAKEFIELD EXPRESS** raised suspicions about a 'former domestic' employed at Hawthorn House.

BACON, ALICE MARTHA, BARONESS BACON OF LEEDS AND NORMANTION

Born in **NORMANTON** in 1909, the daughter of a coalminer, Baroness Bacon was an outstanding MP from 1945 until 1970. Described as 'one of the post-war innovators who helped create the welfare state', she initially began her career as a teacher at an elementary school in **FEATHERSTONE** but soon entered politics becoming the youngest women ever to be elected to the Labour Party's National Executive. In Harold Wilson's government she held the offices of Minister of State for the Home Office and Minister of State for Education and Science. She became a privy councillor in 1966 and was made a life peer. Alice Bacon died in 1993 and was buried in the graveyard at Normanton Parish Church.

BADSWORTH

A still largely rural and popular residential village with a number of architecturally important buildings including St Mary's Church, High Farm, Rockingham Farm and Manor Farm. The inhabitants supported the Royalist cause during the Civil War when, legend has it, the stained glass windows in the church were dismantled and buried for safe-keeping. They were never recovered. From the date of the conflict, almost the whole of the village was owned by the Badsworth Hall estate. This was sold piecemeal in 1926 and the old hall was demolished in 1940, only the arched gateway and stable block surviving. The hall was formerly the home of the celebrated **BADSWORTH HUNT**.

St Mary's Church, Badsworth. LMA

Badsworth Hunt. LMA

BADSWORTH HUNT

One of the oldest and most celebrated foxhunts in the county, founded by Thomas Bright of Badsworth Hall who inherited the estate from his father in 1720. A 'Fox Feast' was held annually in the *Bay Horse Inn* in **WENTBRIDGE** until 1874. One of its most famous masters was Lord Martin Bladen **HAWKE**. The hunt, which famously gave its name to a steam engine and an escort destroyer, was amalgamated with the Bramham Moor Hunt in 2002.

BAGLEY'S CRYSTAL GLASS COMPANY

Founded in 1871 in **KNOTTINGLEY**, the company became a market leader in the inter-war years, producing inexpensive pressed glassware for a mass market. In 1912, the firm expanded its range, manufacturing lead crystal for a period of two years. Demand for the wares increased following the introduction of coloured wares under the 'Crystaltynt' brand in the early 1930s, the patronage of Queen Mary, who bought several wares after display at the British Industries Fair in 1934, boosting sales. In October 1937 King George VI and Queen Elizabeth visited the works and were presented with a Marine Bowl, the royal visit again having a beneficial impact. During the Second World War, Bagley's made beer glasses for the NAAFI to replace thousands lost in breakages. In the 1930s, technicians at the firm routinely used a uranium-rich dye to impart a yellow tint to green glass. After the dropping of the atomic bomb in 1945, three tons of the substance was confiscated! The factory closed in 1975 owing to the lack of skilled labour. It was absorbed by Jackson's, a firm subsequently acquired by Rockware who continue the tradition of producing local glass.

BAINES, WILLIAM

The son of a **HORBURY** organist, this classical composer and concert pianist had a particular affinity with the Yorkshire landscape, compositions such as *Twilight Woods, Paradise Gardens* and *The Lone Wreck* reflecting his love for his native county. He moved to Cleckheaton and York where he was befriended by the Dawson family who gave him the opportunity of developing his talent on their Steinway and Bechstein grand pianos. He died prematurely of tuberculosis at the tender age of twenty-three but left over two hundred compositions including his *Symphony in C Minor* which was first performed at the Grassington Festival in June 1991. He is buried in Horbury cemetery, the nearby congregational church displaying a plaque to his memory.

BANKS, WILLIAM STOTT

A prominent Wakefield solicitor and politician, Banks is best remembered as a pioneering pedestrian, his books *Walks in Yorkshire: the North West and the North East* published in 1866 and *Walks about Wakefield* which appeared in 1871 anticipating the popularity of rambling by almost a century. He also produced the fascinating title *A List of Provincial Words in use in Wakefield* in1865.

BANNICKERS

Coarse linen, knee-length shorts worn by miners.

BANQUET

Always noted for its civic hospitality, the local authority in Wakefield excelled itself on 30 April 1891 when it entertained His Royal Highness The Duke of Clarence and Avondale on the occasion of the opening of the Wakefield Technical and Art School. After a grand procession through the city streets, the cavalcade sat down to a sumptuous meal in the wonderfully decorated Council Chamber. 'In the centre of the royal table was placed large white swans filled with narcissus and lilies of the valley. A novel effect was produced by the introduction of a

Programme for the official visit of the Duke of Clarence. LMA

number of tiny white shoes, each containing a single magnificent rose.' The menu was as follows:

SOUP

Clear Mock-Turtle

FISH

Salmon Hollandaise
Soles in Aspic

ENTRÉE

Mutton Cutlets with Tomatoes

REMOVES

Veal. Sirloin Beef. Quarter Lamb. Roast and Boiled Spring Chickens.
Pigeons in Aspic.
Yorkshire Hams. Ox Tongues. Lobster Salad.

GAME

Leveret Pie. Guinea Fowl. Black Game.

SWEETS

Marischino Jelly. Wine Jelly. Dantzic Jelly. Chartreuse Cream. Moss Cream.
Swiss Cream. German Tarts. Italian Pastry

'The wines were all of the choicest vintages.'

BARING-GOULD, REVEREND SABINE

Curate in 1864 at **HORBURY** Bridge Mission credited as the composer of *Onward Christian Soldiers* and other hymns. Born in Exeter in 1834, he came to Yorkshire to initial ridicule. Mud and stones were flung at his window by youths but he persevered and instituted popular readings. He began a savings club, penning his most famous hymn at Whitsuntide 1865. A novelist whose romances *Through Flood and Flame* and *The Pennycumquicks* portrayed some of the charms of his Yorkshire parish, he also wrote *Yorkshire Oddities*. He died in 1924.

BARMBY, GOODWIN

Reforming firebrand minister at **WAKEFIELD WESTGATE CHAPEL** for twenty-one years between 1858 and 1879. Contemporaries described him as 'an ardent radical from childhood' who is said to have harangued Suffolk labourers on their fundamental rights when he was only a boy of sixteen! He

The Barnsley Canal at Royston, looking towards Ryhill. Brian Elliott Collection

introduced the term 'communism' into the English language well in advance of its common adoption by Marxist ideologists. After a visit to the continent in 1840 he wrote: '...conversed with some of the most advanced minds of the French metropolis and there, in the company of some disciples of Babeuf, then called the Equalitarians, I first pronounced the name of communism which has since ...acquired that worldwide reputation.' Active in local political circles, he became ward chairman of the Liberal Party and he set up a network of Band of Faith churches with branches in Carlisle and London.

BARNSLEY CANAL
Opened in 1799, the eleven-mile waterway linked Barnsley and Wakefield. Mainly horse-drawn barges carried limestone, grain and particularly coal. The canal was abandoned in 1953.

BARSTOW, STAN
Novelist and playwright born, the son of a miner, in **HORBURY** in 1928. One of the 'angry young men' of the period, a leader of the 'realism' movement, this former engineer produced his best-selling novel *A Kind of Loving* in 1960. It captured the mood of the times and in 1962 inspired the

Stan Barstow (extreme right) at the Little Bull *in Ossett.* Wakefield Cultural Services

'kitchen sink' film drama of the same name directed by the legendary John Schlesinger and starring Alan Bates. A stage play followed in 1970. Many of the author's subsequent works are set in the imaginary West Yorkshire town of Cressley. **HORBURY**, settings around Wakefield and local characters inspire much of the prose. The quotation, 'The world may be full of fourth-rate writers, but it's also full of fourth-rate readers', is attributed to Barstow.

BARTHOLOMEW, WILLIAM H

Pioneering and innovative engineer to the **AIRE AND CALDER NAVIGATION**. He introduced and patented the shipment of coal in towed compartment boats known as **TOM PUDDINGS**. Aged only 21, he took over as chief engineer of the company in 1852 following the death of his father Thomas Hamond Bartholomew who is buried within sight of the river in the graveyard adjoining **STANLEY ST PETER'S CHURCH**.

BEAVEN, JOHN ALFRED DISRAELI

This former mathematics master at **WAKEFIELD QUEEN ELIZABETH'S GRAMMAR SCHOOL**, known affectionately to his family as 'Uncle Diz', became a lieutenant in the Royal Artillery during World War Two, serving with the 9th Coast Regiment in the defence of Betang Kusar against the Japanese. He was captured and taken prisoner and put to work on the notorious Burma – Siam Railway where, along with hundreds of comrades, he suffered appalling cruelty. He died of abuse at the age of thirty four in July 1943 and is buried in the Thanbyuzayat War Cemetery.

BED TIMES THIRTY
In a trail blazing experiment, Wakefield led the world in the 1870s by creating the world's largest bed, a carpenter taking his joint inspiration from the table of the fabled Arthurian knights and the dormitory arrangements of a slave ship. He fashioned a giant circular bed to accommodate thirty sleepers in the *Round Robin* lodging house in Westgate. The cost of a berth was 2d per night.

BENNETT, ALAN
This talented writer and playwright enlisted for his National Service in the Yorkshire and Lancashire Regiment in **PONTEFRACT** in 1952. A self-confessed inept soldier whose success as a sniper was only verbal, he later admitted: 'I was not much good with a rifle, so, dreading the recoil, I closed my eyes for a split second before I pressed the trigger.'

BENSON, ROBERT, LORD BINGLEY
The son of Robert Benson of Wakefield who bought an estate at **WRENTHORPE**, Robert Benson II became Chancellor of the Exchequer in 1711 and Ambassador to Madrid in 1713, his experiences of classical Italian architecture developing his talents for art and design. He obtained a number of design commissions in England and built his own mansion at Bramham.

BENTON, JENNET
This so-called 'Wise Woman of Wakefield' lived on the outskirts of the town during the seventeenth century. She was famous for her philtres and love potions. Following an access dispute with her neighbour Richard Jackson who owned Bunny Hall Farm, she was arraigned before York Assizes in 1656 on a charge of witchcraft but was acquitted.

BILLINTON, WILLIAM
Architect and civil engineer, born in 1807, who practiced from offices in Bond Terrace, Wakefield. He was the engineer to the Wakefield Waterworks Company. His most ambitious designs in 1837 were for the largely unexecuted Leeds Zoological Gardens. Only the castellated bear pit in Cardigan Road remains.

BINGHAM, THE REVEREND JOSEPH
A learned and distinguished author whose was born in Wakefield in 1668. He was internationally famous for his work *Origines Ecclesiasticae or the Antiquities*

of the Christian Church in ten volumes. The work was a best-seller and was translated into Latin but its substantial royalties were lost in speculating in the South Sea Bubble. Bingham died shortly after completing the last volume in 1723.

BINGHAM, THE REVEREND JOSHUA

A native of **OSSETT** and originally a supporter of John **WESLEY**, Bingham became disillusioned with Methodist and set up his own Binghamite sect, a movement that has faded into almost total oblivion.

BINNS, BARTHOLOMEW, 'BATH'

Fifth-generation chimney sweep, born as one of eleven children in Bancroft Yard, Wakefield in 1857. His alcoholic father had a famous sign above his door: 'WHO LIVES HERE? WHO DO YOU THINK? BEN BINNS THE SWEEP. GIVE HIM A DRINK' By the age of eight, the boy, whose only encounter with a bathing tub was at his baptism – he screamed – was working five or six hours before he attended school in the afternoon. Like his father, he was a drunkard. He died in 1927.

'Want to buy any soap?' LMA

BISHOPGARTH

Wakefield mansion erected in 1893 on Margaret Street as a residence for the city bishops. In recent years it has become a training centre for officers of **WEST YORKSHIRE POLICE.**

BLACK DEATH

Fearsome and highly contagious plague that ravaged England during the fourteenth century when a third or possibly a half of the population died in the two years between 1348 and 1349. Wakefield lost a third of its citizens to the disease. Church registers show that 130 people died in the town in 1615, 200 succumbing in 1645. The scourge also struck in outlying villages such as **ACKWORTH** where the **PLAGUE STONE** was erected and in **WOOLLEY.**

BLACK LACE

Wakefield pop group who had a dozen hit records between 1979 and 1996.

They also released nine party albums. Nominated by the musical press as The Wally Act of the Year' they produced what are arguably the most nauseating lyrics in the history of popular music. Everyone winces to the words of *Aggadoo*: 'Aaaa gaa, doo doo doo push pineapple shake the tree,' but the song remains a firm favourite with DJ's and audiences particularly at weddings and funerals. The band also produced the wonderfully esoteric and cerebral: *We're Having a Gang Bang.*

BLACK LUNG DISEASE

Respiratory ailment also known as Coal Worker's Pneumoconiosis (CWP) or Anthacosis. The disease tends to affect older, fifty years of age plus workers in the coal mining industry, prolonged exposure to dust causing breathing and heart problems. Emphysema may develop bringing on shortness of breath, enlarged chests and bluish skin discolorations. Badly affected miners may have to resort to nebulisers and oxygen masks. Compensation has been pursued although no major settlements like those awarded for **VIBRATION WHITE FINGER** have been agreed.

BLACK MONK OF PONTEFRACT

Well documented poltergeist who first appeared at 30 East Drive in 1966 and stayed for three years. More mischievous than malevolent, the spectre made a complete nuisance of itself, party-pieces including turning on taps, smashing glass, raising dust and levitating household goods, furniture and food. In September 1968, the *Yorkshire Evening Post* and the *Pontefract and Castleford Express* published exciting features about 'Fred' prompting visits by curious tourists. The poltergeist was described as a monk dressed in a black habit and a cowl, one local historian suggesting that 400 years earlier he had been hanged for rape and murder.

BLACK ROCK

Last port of call on the **WESTGATE RUN**. The pub was opened as the *New Inn* in 1842. Renamed in honour of the area's coal mining tradition in 1886, it was the former home of John **POTTER**.

BLUE BELL INN

This popular hostelry in **WENTBRIDGE** on the **GREAT NORTH ROAD** was a notorious haunt of criminals and outlaws during the seventeenth century, the licensee, who aided and abetted his customers, losing his licence. This was restored in 1633 when a new sign was painted in celebration. Successive landlords preserved this sign until quite recent times. It showed a crudely painted bell and the date 1633.

BOATMEN

Bargees who plied their trade on local rivers and canals in the eighteenth, nineteenth and the early part of the twentieth centuries. A particularly colourful breed of men operated on the Knottingley Cut, their character informing an animated description in Tom Bradbury's delightful book *The Aire* published in 1893: 'There is a lot of unexplored originality about a boatman. One is the classical flow of language in which he indulges. Usually he is of a morose disposition, but occasionally he wakes up and then the verbal fireworks begin to go off. When he is in one of these playful humours he can infuse more monumental emphasis into the remarks he addresses to his crew, which often only consist of his wife and horse, than a healthy man can build up when he jumps out of bed in the dark on the business ends of a lot of tin tacks that his considerate wife has left about in cleaning down. The reckless invention he displays in the choice of expletives is very artistic. It is calculated to kill on sight. A barge properly manned consists of the skipper and his crew. There are two cabins fore and aft. The skipper and his wife sleep in one; the crew and his wife sleep in the other.'

BODY SNATCHERS

In the early nineteenth century, corpses were much in demand by schools of anatomy, so-called 'resurrectionists' digging up bodies and making off with coffins soon after burial. In remote rural areas, watchtowers were built in churchyards to thwart the illicit trade, night-watchmen patrolling streets and graveyards in places like Wakefield. East **ARDSLEY** churchyard was plagued by the menace. On one occasion a regular drinker at the *Old Bull's Head* in the village noticed two sweat-stained men enter the inn with soil on their clothing. Suspicious of their behaviour, he went outside and discovered the cause of their exertions. A corpse disguised in a greatcoat was tied to the seat of a cart. The body was removed and the man took its place with his head bowed, the body snatchers returning and driving off none the wiser towards Tingley. One of the men accidentally touched their passenger and shouted out in alarm. 'Hey! He's warm!' He replied: 'Ye two beggars 'ud be warm if ye'd been where I've been!' Frightened rigid, the two men jumped from the cart and ran off.

BOLLES, THE RIGHT WORSHIPFUL DAME MARY

Born about 1579, she lived in some splendour in **HEATH OLD HALL**. She died there in 1662. She left a £500 legacy for the instruction of Wakefield apprentices and £120 for the entertainment of mourners at her funeral. Thereafter, she haunted her old home, as a consequence of unfulfilled stipulations in her carefully crafted will. There is a chilling depth in the river below the old hall known as the Bolles Pit.

BOLLES WATER TOWER

Picturesquely surviving at Heath, the tower dates from the 1700s. Built over a hillside spring, it utilised the flow to turn an 18 feet waterwheel that supplied water to **HEATH OLD HALL** and its village. A marvel in early hydraulic engineering, it may have been connected by a suspended conduit lined with lead to a surviving storage cistern. This was built alongside the hall's gatehouse in similar style to the tower. It bears Lady Bolles's coat of arms.

BOOTH, JOSEPH AND FRANCIS

Father and son organ builders. Joseph was trained as a plumber but was fascinated by sound. Under the guidance of Joseph Priestley, he built a model organ and went on to invent a pneumatic action in Wakefield, his magnificent instrument in the Brunswick Wesleyan Chapel in Leeds receiving instant acclaim. Francis relocated to a purpose built factory in Howard Street in 1857 and produced fine organs for customers home and abroad – fifteen went to the West Indies! He was a noted organist and a friend of Charles **WATERTON** whose nieces attended the Howard Street premises for lessons.

BOOTLEG

Disorderly pauper John Hutchings completed his stretch in **WAKEFIELD PRISON** in August 1906 and walked out a free man. He marched up Westgate and stole a shovel from the ironmongery store of Beaumont and Savile in Cross Square and was immediately arrested. He told the magistrate, who jailed him for fourteen days with hard labour, 'I stole it because I could not walk in these boots and would sooner be in prison.'

Relief at last. LMA

BOTTOMBOAT

Ancient settlement near **STANLEY** above a loop in the **CALDER RIVER**. It has been known by its current name since at least 1709, the reference alluding to two ferry boats that operated from **ALTOFTS** – the Topboat - and **STANLEY** – the Bottomboat. The first ferries sailed in 1605 when the owner of the service lived in the *Ferry Boat Inn*. In 1672, the ferry boat capsized, drowning ten passengers. In harsh winters, visitors came from far and wide to skate on the frozen Calder in a locality known as 'The Pastures'. Always lively and colourful, the village once enjoyed its Good Husband Street and several fun addresses with names like Holy Row, Casey Court and Toad Hole.

BOYCOTT, GEOFFREY

Renowned Yorkshire and England cricketer, one of the best batsmen in the history of the game who became the Wisden Cricketer of the Year in 1965. He was born in 1940 in Fitzwilliam. The gifted right-handed batsman was one of the finest technicians of the age, a man who guarded his wicket with rare tenacity and total commitment. He was never a swashbuckling innings maker but his stoical, immoveable style earned a consistent place in the Headingley side and in 1964 he made his international Test debut against Australia, playing for England – he absented himself from thirty Tests –in one hundred and eight Tests until 1982 when he batted against India. He notched up his one hundredth century against Australia in the 4th Test at Headingley in 1977. In 1977 he became the only England player to bat on all five days of a Test. Stubborn and self-centred, he demonstrated typical Yorkshire bluffness and alienated himself to many in the game. After stumps were pulled, he became a popular commentator on radio and television but an incident in a hotel in the French resort of Antibes in 1996, blighted his career. He stayed there with his girlfriend Margaret Moore and the couple spent the evening sipping champagne in the company of American rock star Billy Joel. Afterwards, they retired to their room where they fell into a heated conversation about marriage. Moore sustained head injuries and involved the police, alleging assault. Boycott denied punching Moore twenty times but was found guilty and was given a three month suspended sentence and fined 50,000 francs. He challenged the verdict but lost the appeal. He was immediately dropped by BSkyB and the BBC and the *Sun* newspaper ended his contract as a columnist. He has since made a media comeback.

BRABBEN, HILDA

Scriptwriter from **CASTLEFORD** who composed most of the scripts for the 1952 hit children's TV programme *The Flowerpot Men*. Her famous characters Bill and Ben and Little Weed were inspired by her mischievous brothers William and Benjamin and their sister Phyllis. Brabben introduced 'flobberdob' language into the national lexicon.

BRADBURY, TOM
Child prodigy who developed a talent for satirical wit and eccentric conduct. He was born in Wakefield in 1677, his attendance in **ALVERTHORPE** church introducing him to the power of oratory. He began preaching to some ridicule and scorn at the age of eighteen, his use of the anecdote and the political joke bringing forth mirth and amusement in his congregations but drawing reprimand from the church authorities. 'I have seen Mr. Bradbury's 'Sermons', wrote one commentator, 'the nonsense and buffoonery of which would make one laugh, if the wretched insults over the pious dead did not make one tremble.' The religious establishment tended to scorn his lack of a sacred calling and he was despised and threatened with death. The intended assassin was told to attend the speaker's sermons and to hatch a murder plot. He was so captivated by the force of the homily, however, that he abandoned his scheme, admitted his evil intent and was converted. A jovial and convivial man, Bradbury grew rich and died in 1759.

BRADFORD HALL
Ancient manor house in **STANLEY** situated on the site of the present **CLARKE HALL**. The property was the home of successive generations of the Bradford family from 1437 when the estate was bought by William Bradford of Heath. Timber-framed, the hall had a sumptuous parlour with an exquisite plaster ceiling caparisoned with roundels, fleur-de-lis and gadrooned bosses.

BRADLEY, GEORGE
Prominent lawyer and property speculator whose business empire brought him the twin approbations 'Mr Castleford' and 'Mr Featherstone'. He developed interests in both towns and built a commodious home in **CASTLEFORD**, which became the *North Eastern Hotel*. He bought Aketon Hall in 1866.

BRADLEY, THOMAS
Chaplain to King Charles I born in either 1596 or 1597. He sympathetically attended the execution of the sovereign in 1649, drawing the wrath of the Parliamentarians who evicted him and his family from his home in **ACKWORTH**. Regaining his property at the Restoration, he built two almshouses for poor widows near the village green in 1666 and refurbished the font in St Cuthbert's Church which has a monument to his name. He died in 1673.

BRAMHALL, ARCHBISHOP JOHN

Born in **PONTEFRACT** around 1593 – he attended **PONTEFRACT KING'S SCHOOL** - the eminent prelate became chaplain to the Archbishop of York. In 1630 he went to Ireland were he was employed as Lord Wentworth's chaplain, afterwards becoming Bishop of London. Indicted for treason, he was imprisoned in Dublin but released. Wisely, he fled to the continent during the Civil War, returning afterwards to become Archbishop of Armagh. He died in Dublin in 1663. He was the author of *The History of Hull*.

BRASS BAND

Wakefield District has seven brass bands affiliated to the Yorkshire and Humberside Brass Band Association – a lively 14 per cent. Brass bands are very much a part of the local culture. Mining is the bedrock of much of the local brass band tradition although pioneering bands like Gawthorpe Brass 85 have widened the appeal of the music to the wide community. In 1931, the Stanley and Newmarket Colliery Band broke with tradition when ten-year-old Iris Holdgate became the first female member of a brass band to compete in a national finals competition in London. In 2002 Frickley and South Elmsall Brass Band gained first place in the National Mineworkers Championships in Blackpool.

BRETTON HALL

Imposing nine-bayed mansion built for Sir William Wentworth in 1720 and adapted for Colonel Beaumont in 1815. Situated in the grounds of the **YORKSHIRE SCULPTURE PARK**, it is now used by **BRETTON HALL UNIVERSITY COLLEGE** as an arts academy.

Bretton Hall. LMA

BRETTON HALL UNIVERSITY COLLEGE

Specialist arts centre founded in 1949 and currently on three sites – Manygates, Wakefield, Bretton Hall Campus in West Bretton and the Lodge in Kettlethorpe. Following budget cuts the College will be closed and sold in 2007 when students will be assimilated into the University of Leeds.

BRIGGS, HENRY

Born in 1797, he became a mining pioneer, developing pits at **FLOCKTON** and **WHITWOOD** during the 1830s. From a colliery owning family, he was one of the first industrialists to introduce the notion of profit sharing. A visionary, he introduced workers discussion groups and provided a sports ground and a theatre for his employees. He died in 1868.

BRIGHT, SIR JOHN

Prominent Parliamentarian during the Civil War who served as a colonel under Cromwell in Scotland and in various other military campaigns. He was involved in the siege of **PONTEFRACT CASTLE**. After the conflict he became an able MP and served as the High Sheriff of Yorkshire. He lived in some style in **BADSWORTH**, four financially advantageous marriages securing him a large fortune. Bright died in 1688, a surgeon removing 'two stones out of his bladder, which weighed near four ounces.' He has an opulent memorial in Badsworth church.

BRONTË, CHARLOTTE

This famous author of *Jane Eyre* became the wife of Arthur Bell Nicholls, the vicar of Kirk Smeaton, a village south of **PONTEFRACT**.

BROTHERHOOD OF MAN

Pop group with Wakefield connections, Sandra Stevens and Martin Lee hailing from the town. The group famously won the Eurovision Song Contest with *Save Your Kisses For Me* an internationally popular melody that even eclipsed Abba's *Waterloo*. The song became a number one hit in thirty-four countries and one of the five best selling singles of the 1970s in the UK.

BROTHERTON, EDWARD ALLEN, LORD BROTHERTON OF WAKEFIELD

A quick-witted Manchester man, Brotherton had an idea for utilising waste products from the gas industry. Borrowing money from relatives in Wakefield, he set up an ammonia plant in Calder Vale Road, Wakefield in 1878. His business boomed and in 1882, a further plant was opened in Leeds. By 1902, Brotherton was the Mayor of Wakefield, his business empire expanding to Birmingham, Liverpool, Rothwell Haigh and Stockport. In 1904, he established the Brotherton Trust with £9,000 to assist the poor pensioners of Wakefield. Two years before he died in 1930, he became Lord Brotherton of Wakefield.

BURBERRY
Luxury upper-crust fashion label. Garments designed for couture customers in London, Paris and New York are manufactured using the trademark plaid in Coronation Mills in **CASTLEFORD**.

BUNNY, RICHARD
Born in 1514, he was the son of a country gentleman and entrepreneur who developed some of the first coal mines in the area around the family seat of Bunny Hall on the outskirts of Wakefield. He inherited his father's estate at the age of twenty-one and became a royal courtier and an MP in 1547. In that year he purchased the predecessor building to **NEWLAND HALL** and obtained a number of sinecures from the crown. A Protestant, he fled to Switzerland during the reign of Queen Mary, partly to avoid arrest for forgery. He was pardoned in 1574 and returned to live quietly at Newland until his death in 1584.

BUTTY MONEY
Advance on miners' wages paid, for example, when work on an unproductive seam yielded little coal. Workers were paid on shift output.

BYATT, A S
Novelist who spent part of her childhood in **PONTEFRACT**. Her recollections of the town's castle surface in some of the passages in her 1990 novel *Possession*.

C

CALDER RIVER
Rising in the Pennine hills above Todmorden, the Calder enters the district at **HORBURY** and flows through Wakefield for a further 12½ miles via **KIRKTHORPE, STANLEY** and **BOTTOMBOAT** to the confluence with the **AIRE RIVER** in **CASTLEFORD**.

CARLETON GRANGE
Based on an earlier house, the mansion was re-modelled by influential banker Thomas William **TEW** around 1879. It is noted for its exquisite plasterwork, carvings and stained glass windows. The mansion was once packed with treasures including pictures, pottery, coins and antiquities.

CARR GATE

Former hamlet and highway access point at the edge of the densely wooded Wakefield **OUTWOOD**. Close by is **WROE'S MANSION**, which is now an Elim Pentecostal Church residential home.

CARR, JOHN

One of the most eminent provincial architects of the eighteenth century, he was born at **HORBURY** in 1723, the son of a stonemason. He grew up a journeyman in his father's employ. His first public commission, completed in 1754, was the racecourse grandstand on York's Knavesmire, the achievement bringing instant aristocratic acclaim. Carr married a member of the Lascelles family and when wealthy Henry Lascelles set forth his proposals for a magnificent mansion at Harewood, he was asked to produce a design, the work commencing in 1759. He went on to produce scores of designs for buildings which continue to enhance the Yorkshire and national landscapes, his successes including Constable Burton Hall, near Leyburn (1762-68), Thornes House, Wakefield (1779), the Crescent at Buxton (1779-84) and the new bridge at **FERRYBRIDGE** (1797). In addition, he completed a structural survey of York Minster and was the architect for a number of that city's mansions. In 1790, 'as a monument at once of his skill and bounty' he built a handsome church in his native town saying during construction: 'I am not ashamed of its being known that I had once been poor. I have many a time had to lie in bed whilst my breeches were mending.' Carr became Lord Mayor of York in 1770 and 1785. In 1791 he was one of only four provincial architects to be elected to honorary membership of the London Architects Club. Carr had an excellent singing voice and in 1789 he sang for the Prince of Wales and his brother, delivering a stirring rendition in York of *Hearts of Oak*. Carr amassed a fortune estimated to have been worth £150,000 when he died at the grand old age of 84 in 1807. He is buried in Horbury's church of St Peter and St Leonard, which he built as his own expense (£8000).

CARTWRIGHT, EDMUND

An inventive mechanical engineer, born in 1743 at Marnham in Nottinghamshire, Edmund was the fourth of four sons. His early education, to the age of fourteen, was at **WAKEFIELD QUEEN ELIZABETH'S GRAMMAR SCHOOL**. A brilliant scholar, he went up to Oxford and studied theology, becoming a rector more

Edmund Cartwright, 1743-1823, textile machine inventor.
Brian Elliott Collection

attuned to the Muses of poetry and literature than the Gods of fire and flame. In 1784, he visited one of Arkwright's cotton spinning mills and was fired in the determination that he could adapt the spinning technology to benefit weaving. His first prototypes were crude and inefficient but, after initial set-backs, he produced the world's first commercially viable powered loom – one of the most important machines to inspire the Industrial Revolution. Cartwright's first weaving shed was built in Doncaster. It proved an instant success. The career inventor designed everything from fireproof floorboards to inter-locking bricks and a machine for making ropes. One of his brothers pursued a successful naval career, becoming a major in the army. Another became a notable fur trapper in Canada with the nickname 'Labrador Cartwright'. Edmund Cartwright died in 1823.

CASTLE, BARBARA

This gritty and able Labour politician and Cabinet member spent part of her early childhood in Love Lane in **PONTEFRACT**, later moving to Carleton. She was educated at Love Lane Elementary School and Pontefract and District Girls' High School. She became an MP in 1945 and was a Euro MP between 1979 and 1989. After a colourful lifetime in politics, she was made a life peer in 1990, taking the title Baroness Castle of Blackburn.

CASTLEFORD

Industrial town founded as *Legioleum* or *Lagentium* by the Romans at a strategic fording point at the confluence of the **AIRE RIVER** and the **CALDER RIVER**. The Lock Lane Bridge was built in 1808. The town developed as a centre for glassmaking and in the 1850s the bottle industry provided containers for sauces, medicines and beer and employed a third of the local population. Production topped twenty million bottles per year. The town also produced earthenware pottery, the **DUNDERDALE** brand being the most famous. Clothing and chemical manufacture and especially coal mining – there were twenty-one pits in the area in 1964 – became prominent. During the Second World War, the town had the unenviable distinction of being dubbed '*the most populated square mile in the British Isles.*' With the demise of the colliery industry in the 1980s, six pitheads were abandoned causing large-scale unemployment. The world famous sculptor Henry **MOORE** was born in the town in 1898. The flour milling company **ALLINSON** operate on a riverside site that has been occupied since ancient times. **HICKSON AND WELCH** produce chemicals and fashion icon **BURBERRY** manufacture prestige clothing from a factory in Albion Street. The ebullient spirit of Castlefordians – many now work in the retail and leisure developments situated along the nearby M62 corridor – is exemplified by the local rugby league team – the **CASTLEFORD TIGERS LEAGUE FOOTBALL CLUB**.

CASTLEFORD BRIDGE

The town's oldest structure erected in 1808 and often referred to as 'Hartley's Bridge' in honour of the **PONTEFRACT** civil engineers Bernard and Jesse **HARTLEY**. The surviving steps at the foot of the bridge were used by river passengers disembarking from Goole. Passengers travelled on to Leeds by coach to avoid the tedious necessity of negotiating a host of locks upstream. In 1856, effigies of Edgar Brefitt, the detested owner of the Aire and Calder Glass Bottle Works, and his manager were burnt and thrown over the bridge wall. The image of the bridge appears on pottery made in the town.

CASTLEFORD FORUM

Befitting the town's Roman origins and the capacity of its residents for a good chinwag, this rendezvous point and outdoor Parliament stood at the junction of Aire Street and Bridge Street near the bridge, consisting of a gas lamp and direction signs projecting from a plinth of two circular stones. It was a focal point from the early 1800s until the mid 1960s - a favourite hustings perch for local politicians. Ordinary mortals would smoke a pipe here …and wait for the pubs to open!

CASTLEFORD TIGERS RUGBY LEAGUE FOOTBALL CLUB

Super League rugby team who play at the Wheldon Road ground now known as The Jungle. Consistently in the top flight, the club was founded in 1926, winning the coveted Yorkshire League in 1932 and their first of four Challenge Cups in 1935. Famous players include recent stars Kevin and Bob Beardmore, Keith Hepworth, John Joyner and Brian Lockwood.

Castleford Tigers Rugby League FC.
From Wakefield MDC's official guide.

CASTLEFORD TOWN ASSOCIATION FOOTBALL CLUB

Local affinities with the round ball have long since been squashed, but for a while in the early 1900s, the local football team vied with Sheffield United, Nottingham Forest and Hull City for supremacy. The club was established in the 1880s. Its best season was in 1919/20 when it finished 7th in the league. A few years later, it 'took the football world by storm' in its glorious achievements in the forerunner to the FA Cup. Away to Bradford Park Avenue of the First Division before a crowd of 10,690 (the team took 2000 supporters) the team was narrowly defeated 3-2. Two seasons later in 1928, the Third Division was created but the club was mysteriously denied admission, local anecdotes suggesting that either the ground was too far away from the railway station…or there was a lack of palm-greasing! Subsequently, the club went into decline and withdrew from the league, the ground being sold to the local rugby league club. Oh what might have been! Town had a galaxy of stars including goalkeeper Harold Gough who went on to play for Sheffield United and England and Welsh international Harold Millership.

CASTLEFORD WOMEN
Castleford women must needs be fair, because they wash both in Calder and Aire. (Old Yorkshire folk rhyme)

CASTLEFORD WOMEN'S CENTRE
Pioneering training and empowerment initiative dedicated to life improvements among the disadvantaged women of the **CASTLEFORD** area. The centre has developed a deserved reputation for innovation and excellence and has become an international model for lifelong learning.

CAWOOD, STEPHEN
Staunch Parliamentarian owner of Cawood House, **EAST HARDWICK**. He endowed the Cawood Trust with eighty-four acres of land, funds providing a school for poor children. Cawood House was demolished in 1964.

CHALMERS, ANDREW
A learned Scotsman from Hythie, near Fetterangus, Chalmers came south in 1880 as the minister of **WAKEFIELD WESTGATE CHAPEL**. A canny man, he married the local daughter of prominent worsted spinner W T Marriott, his father-in-law building the couple an elegant house in Blenheim Road. Chalmers immersed himself in local affairs, lecturing in the Mechanics' Institute, sitting on the governing board of Clayton Hospital and writing a history of his own church. In 1894 he donated money for the establishment of a church institute in Fetterangus, supplying 1600 books for its library. He wrote hymns, chants and litanies for his own congregation. He died in 1912, a chapel bust at the foot of his pulpit remembering his twenty-eight years service.

CHANTRY BRIDGE CHAPEL, WAKEFIELD
The best of only four surviving Middle Ages bridge chapels in England (they were partly built as shrines to attract tolls for the upkeep of the river crossings) the chapel (one of four similar chapels in Wakefield – see **SAINT MARY MAGDALENE CHAPEL, SAINT SWITHINS CHAPEL** and **SAINT JOHN THE BAPTIST CHAPEL**) originally dates from around 1350. Just

Chantry Bridge Chapel. LMA

200 years later it was badly defaced and was heavily restored in the nineteenth century by the celebrated architect Sir Gilbert Scott, the badly corroded façade being relocated to **KETTLETHORPE HALL** where it was used to front a boat-house and summer-house beside a lake. Erosion further degraded the building and in 1940 a third façade was commissioned incorporating five bays with three small doorways and exquisite parapet reliefs showing various Bible scenes. The chapel is the subject of a large canvas of 1793 by the artist Phillip Reinagle exhibited in **WAKEFIELD ART GALLERY**.

THE ROTARY CLUB OF WAKEFIELD CHANTRY

WAKEFIELD BRIDGE AND CHANTRY CHAPEL

This stone bridge,built soon after 1342, replaced an earlier bridge over the River Calder. The packhorse bridge was added in 1730.The Chantry Chapel of St.Mary, built between 1342 and 1356 is one of only 4 bridge chapels still surviving in England.It was restored in 1847 and more recently.

CHAPELTHORPE
Settlement south of the city defined by the parish of St James. Its clergy would, interspersed by prayer, annually 'beat the bounds' by novelly 'bumping' choir boys on the boundary stones and thrashing hedgerows with willow sprigs.

Lodge at Chevet Moorgate, 1976. Brian Elliott Collection

CHEVET HALL

Rebuilt in 1529 at the centre of a sporting estate that encompassed 2,340 acres including the pond at **NEWMILLERDAM**, the property was bought by the Pilkington family in 1765, gamekeepers setting mantraps for poachers. The gamekeepers were housed in nine strategically placed lodges. The family coat of arms can still be seen on the West Lodge, although the hall was demolished in the 1960s as a consequence of mining subsidence. The estate was purchased by Wakefield Council in 1949 and the grounds have since been incorporated into a country park.

CHILDS, SAMUEL CANNING

Wakefield-born benefactor who made a fortune in the United States. He left Wakefield at the age of six with his father and set up a successful grocery store, adding an 's' to his surname and creating a retail empire that became Acme Markets and The American Food Store company with outlets across several states. He generously provided money for Wakefield's Clayton Hospital's outpatients block also subscribing to the West Jersey Hospital and the Cooper Hospital in his adopted country and a medical centre in Vienna. His munificence was honoured in his birthplace in 1928, when he joined the exalted **HONORARY FREEMEN OF WAKEFIELD**.

CHOLERA

Wakefield suffered a major epidemic of the virulent water borne disease in 1849. The death toll was eighty-seven. In the nearby **WEST RIDING PAUPER LUNATIC ASYLUM,** 106 patients died. Potable water described as containing: 'small animals discernible to the naked eye' was contaminated with raw sewage leaking from cesspits and latrines adjacent to the packed tenements in the slum yards.

CHRIST'S THORN

Thomas Percy, Third Earl of Northumberland had been the champion of Mary Queen of Scots. She gave the earl a holy relic – a thorn from the crown of Christ. Shortly before his own execution in 1572, he gave the relic in turn to his daughter Elizabeth Percy who married Richard Woodrove of **WOOLLEY**. (The Woodrove's were connected with the village from the thirteenth century and lived at the Hall from 1490 until 1599.) The precious thorn was set in a golden cross and kept in the village for some years until it was bequeathed to Elizabeth's confessor, a Jesuit priest by the name of Father Gerard. He reverently removed it from its golden case and placed it inside a crystal cylinder almost hidden by a cone of pearls. This was enclosed in a golden reliquary decorated with multi-coloured enamels. After many adventurers abroad, the reliquary was given in 1803 to Stonyhurst College. It is inscribed in Latin.

Seventeenth century role play at Clarke Hall. LMA

CLARKE HALL

Situated in **STANLEY**, a charming early brick house of 1542 - on the site of **BRADFORD HALL** - with 1629 enlargements. It has an inviting great chamber and a parlour and was once moated, having a secret passage off a door behind the fireplace in the entrance hall, leading to **HEATH HALL**. Its dining hall was once described as being the finest of its type in Yorkshire. 'More impressive, however, is the magnificent plaster ceiling. This unique feature bears a design of Indian corn plants, flowers and scrolls, motifs probably copied from the chintzes imported by the East India Company then being fostered by Charles II.' When Queen Mary visited the hall in September 1936, she particularly admired the ceiling. The Hall was once owned by an ancestor of Sir John **PILKINGTON** and by William **SHAW**. It was extensively restored between 1971 and 1973 and is now used as an educational museum, students taking part in seventeenth century role play. It is open to the public at certain times.

CLARKS BREWERY

Independent real ale brewery established in 1906 off Westgate in Wakefield with its own adjacent public house – *Henry Boons* together with a small number of other tied houses. Ales include Ram's Revenge, Golden Hornet and Mulberry Tree commemorating the famous bush in **WAKEFIELD PRISON**.

CLARKSON, HENRY

Land valuer and surveyor, businessman and speculator who lived at **ALVERTHORPE HALL** from 1864 until 1875. His father owned a woollen mill on Alverthorpe Road, the mill once attracting threats by Luddites. Clarkson carried out a cartographic survey of 300 square miles of land around **BADSWORTH**, and, in association with fellow originator John Walker, a map was published in 1825. He surveyed a route for the **TURNPIKE ROAD** between Wakefield and Denby in 1824, improvements to the **GREAT NORTH ROAD** and surveys for the burgeoning railway system also claiming his attention. Clarkson is best known for his book *Memories of Merrie Wakefield* published in 1887. It describes his life at the hall and gives a fascinating insight into the local history of the period.

CLAY, CHARLES

A wealthy farmer and agricultural implement maker, Clay lived in a large house known as Walton Grange near Wakefield. In 1862, he transferred his business to Stennard Island on the Calder where he successfully manufactured patented horse and steam powered cultivators, horse hoes, chain harrows and other farming tools. He also made road rollers. His innovative implements were employed all over England and he gained a national reputation becoming a founder member of the Central Chamber of Agriculture. Locally, he was a director of the Wakefield Corn Exchange Company.

CLAYTON, IAN

Broad Yorkshire accented, immensely friendly and chirpy **FEATHERSTONE** lad, a noted author, performer and TV celebrity fronting shows such as ITV's

Tonight and *My Yorkshire*. He co-wrote a sterling tribute to **RUGBY LEAGUE** *When Push Comes to Shove.*

CLAYTON, THOMAS

Son of a Wakefield tallow chandler born in 1786, Clayton made a fortune in business and retired to a life of philanthropic endeavour. He donated funds to establish a hospital that bore his name in Wentworth Street and left a £300 per year legacy for its upkeep when he died in 1868.

CLUNIAC MONKS

The most important ecclesiastical order in **PONTEFRACT** established in the Priory of St John founded in the early eleventh century by Robert, son of Ilbert de Lacy. In 1279, the house accommodated a prior and twenty-six brethren 'living honest and commendable lives.' The priory was dissolved in 1539.

COAL GAS

According to local anecdote, a rector at **CROFTON** first discovered the properties of coal gas as an illuminant in the seventeenth century.

COBBLERS HALL, HEATH

Mansion started by a shoemaker with limited funds in the early part of the eighteenth century. The shoemaker could not afford to finish the building, which became colloquially known as Cobblers Hall. In 1740 it was developed by Joseph Randall as an elite school for the education of young noblemen and children of the upper classes. He offered single rooms and the opportunity to be 'boarded, found with tea, sup at private table with the family, and to be taught by the best masters the ancient and modern languages, the mathematics and natural philosophy, fortification and gunnery, moral philosophy, logic and metaphysics; with dancing, fencing, music and drawing for £35 a year.' In advance of its time, the academy failed in 1754.

COBDEN, RICHARD

This able MP for the **WEST RIDING OF YORKSHIRE**, was one of the main advocates for repealing the detested Corn Laws and was an exceptionally motivated and honest politician who brought immense skill and dignity to his office. The Mother of Parliaments was elevated by his presence. In 1815 a Corn Law was passed prohibiting the importation of foreign grain until the price of home-grown corn had reached 80 shillings a quarter. The measure was intended to protect farmers and landowners from falling prices driven low by cheap imports. The legislation had the effect of keeping bread prices high and it did little to raise agricultural wages, the rising manufacturing classes also resenting the protectionism afforded to landlords. There was much tinkering with the legislation over the following decades but, year on year, a mounting anger particularly in Wakefield, whose trade in **CORN**, at certain times of the year, exceeded that of London. Local parliamentary representative Richard Cobden took up the cudgels. Prime Minister Robert Peel had initially steadfastly defended the Corn Laws but under the eloquent onslaught of Cobden, he relented. There is a famous story of him listening to an impassioned speech on repeal by the Right Honourable Member for the West Riding of Yorkshire and taking notes. Overwhelmed by the persuasive force of the argument, he turned to a colleague and said: 'You answer this: I cannot.' When the repealing legislation was passed, Peel spoke highly of his fellow member, Hansard recording thus: 'The name which ought to be, and will be associated with the success of those measures, is the name of one who, acting I believe from pure and disinterested motives, has, with untiring energy, made appeals with an eloquence the more to be admired because it was unaffected and unadorned: the name which ought to be chiefly associated with the success of those measures is the name of Richard Cobden.' Disraeli similarly praised Cobden upon his death in 1865, his eulogy stirring the blood to this day. 'There is something mournful in the history of this Parliament, when we remember how many of our most eminent and valued public men have passed from amongst us. I cannot refer to the history of any other Parliament which will bear to posterity so fatal a record. But there is this consolation, when we remember these unequalled and irreparable visitations – that these great men are not altogether lost to us; that their opinions will be often quoted in this House, their authority appealed to, their judgements attested; even their very words will form part of our discussions and debates. There are some members of Parliament who, though not present in the body, are still members of this House, independent of dissolutions, of the caprice of constituencies, and even of the course of time. I think, Sir, Mr Cobden was one of those men.'

COCKS AND CROWS

In the depths of the Wakefield countryside in 1993, something stirred, a strident call ushering in a new dawn. Reveille has always been thus in the great outdoors, this most organic of alarms springing ordinary folk from their cots with a smile. Not so some new breeds of men. Ungodly hours and cockcrows may be bedfellows in the country but the rudely-awaken commuters of **NETHERTON** were determined to stick several socks in the beaks. Enter Wakefield MDC, a lynch mob of lawyers and a Noise Abatement Order. The Order was served on the cock-keeper at his Strands Lane Farm on 1 April. Quite naturally, he assumed the missive was a wind-up, suggesting that 'the cuckoos round here make more noise than my cockerels'.' But the farmer soon realised that the authority was deadly serious. Months later the case was heard in the magistrates court, the learned adjudicator finding, after a three-day marathon, in favour of the birds. And the council was ordered to pay the cockerels' legal fees ...£14,500 plus VAT. The magnanimous farmer, through his solicitor, offered an olive branch to neighbours inviting them round for lunch. 'Bu it won't be cockerel on the menu', added the brief.

CO-OPS

The movement was inspired by the Rochdale Pioneers who radically sought to end the exploitation of the working classes by unscrupulous traders in provisions and household goods. In the mid-nineteenth century, they set up democratically controlled businesses to retail goods at market prices, selling to members who would secure a year-end dividend calculated in accordance to their purchases. The idea was simple and it worked despite the attempt of some shopkeepers to boycott the movement. Friendly co-ops were established with vigour in Wakefield and in nearly every sizeable town and village across the district. Typically, the emporium in Dale Street **OSSETT** was opened in 1861. So good was business, that in 1869, the manager decided to buy a horse and cart! A survey of the society's accounts shows that the first female employee – a dressmaker earning 21 shillings per week – was engaged in 1885. In that same year, an apprentice cobbler was taken on ...wages in the first year being 3 shillings per week rising to 11 shillings in the fifth year. In 1874, a branch was tentatively opened in West **ARDSLEY**. It was designed so that if the business failed, the premises could be readily converted to residential use. It flourished. Wakefield had its own prestigious store, an angular, multi-windowed extravagance on Smyth Street opened in 1878 in a building now known as Unity House. Remember the friendly service? The assistants wrapped perishable goods up for you in greaseproof paper. Remember the butter in barrels? Remember your Dividend Number?

CORAM, CAPTAIN THOMAS

Born in 1668 with one of the most restive social consciences of the age, Coram worked tirelessly to end the suffering of destitute orphan bastard babies in the largely apathetic and cruel London of the 1720s and 30s. He strived and persuaded with little money of his own to change attitudes over seventeen long years, once complaining of the city's rich: 'I could no more prevail with them than if I had asked them to pull down their breeches and present their backsides to the King and Queen.' Eventually, his stubborn resolution paid off and he recruited supporters to his cause, notably Hogarth and Handel. With their help and the grant of a charter by George II, he established a centre for the care and education of abandoned children. Handel left the rights of his masterpiece *The Messiah* to support the hospital. This was

Captain Thomas Coram, 1668-1751.
Brian Elliott Collection

built as the Foundling Hospital in Lambs Conduit Fields, the charity surviving to this day. The original site of the hospital is now a children's playground called 'Coram's Fields'. Coram died in 1751 but by 1756, his institution was caring for so many children that six 'county outposts' were built. One of these hospitals was in Yorkshire, the establishment eventually becoming **ACKWORTH SCHOOL**. There is some suggestion that the choice of locality was influenced by the observations of meteorologist Luke **HOWARD** who concluded that the climate hereabouts was especially suitable for invalids. When the children arrived in Yorkshire, they were fostered out to wet-nurses in **ACKWORTH, HEMSWORTH, BADSWORTH** and **PONTEFRACT**. In its lifetime, the hospital cared for 2665 children. In 1773, Parliament withdrew its grant and the hospital closed after only twelve years. One of the main reasons for this was the excessive mortality rate, the majority of the young inmates dying before the age of eight. There was great difficulty in obtaining competent nurses and 'humane masters' and the foundling death toll through the contraction of disease was alarming. In 1765, twenty-three children died of dysentery. Smallpox claimed eighteen, fever four, consumption two and other causes five. The disused buildings were purchased by Yorkshire philanthropist Doctor John **FOTHERGILL**.

CORN

Wakefield was a major northern market for corn for centuries. During shortages in 1740, rampaging rioters from Lancashire entered the town with violent intent and their leaders were arrested. In the 1840s, Wakefield traded the largest tonnage of corn outside London, over 300 barges carrying between 50 and 90 tons supplying vast riverside warehouses. A corn market was held every Friday. Such was the clamour of business that the Corn Exchange erected in 1823 was swamped with buyers, prompting the need for a second mart, which was erected in 1837. The demolished Corn Exchange was described by Sir Nikolas Pevsner, the eminent architectural historian, as 'the best building in Wakefield.'

CORRUPTION
Wakefield Parliamentary Borough had the blackest reputation as the most consistently bad in the country in the period between 1850 and 1870 as a consequence of unparalleled bribery, corruption and intimidation.

CORSELLIS, CHARLES, CAESAR
Eminently qualified physician who became the medical director of the **WEST RIDING PAUPER LUNATIC ASYLUM** in 1831, his wife becoming its matron. When the asylum opened in 1818, the prevalent treatments for mental illness were crude and barbaric, outrageous acts such as excessive purging and bleeding and ritualised beating being the norm. Acting on the enlightened policies of his predecessor, the new director introduced dozens of reforms, kindness and therapies based on gainful and instructive employment taking the place of restraining straps and whips. The director was criticised by Doctor Caleb **CROWTHER** who insisted that the asylum should be run by a medical board and honorary physicians like himself. Corsellis was, however, supported by the Commissioners on Lunacy, the asylum being recognised as one of the best three in the country in 1844. He officially quit his post in 1853 citing ill health but constant sniping probably sped his departure.

COUNCIL HOUSES
The first Wakefield council (or corporation houses as they were known then) were begun in 1919 at Elm Tree Street, Belle Vue and Rufford Street off Alverthorpe Road. The showpiece Lupset Estate had over 2000 modern houses and a row of shops, local celebrities giving their names to Waterton Road, Gissing Road and Robin Hood Crescent.

COUNTY GENERAL HOSPITAL
Opened in Park Hills, Wakefield in 1899, the hospital was intended to provide medical facilities for the 'sick poor of the working classes', providing 150 beds. The hospital had every modern facility including spring mattresses and an innovative ventilation system that washed and humidified air maintained at a constant temperature of 65 degrees. During the Great War, the facility attended 1192 wounded soldiers. The hospital was eventually absorbed into the National Health Service.

COXLEY VALLEY
Wooded beauty spot west of **NETHERTON** famous for its annual show of bluebells.

CRAVEN, JOHN

Innovative Wakefield engineer and brick maker with works on Dewsbury Road. He designed the revolutionary 'stiff plastic' process brick making machine. This pressed and moulded hard clays and shales to produce strong and dense bricks that required minimal drying. In 1862, inspired by German enterprise, he installed the first Hoffman Continuous Kiln in England, its twelve brick-hardening chambers, producing superior bricks and reducing prices.

CRAWSHAY, RICHARD

Known to posterity as 'The Iron King of Wales' this canny Yorkshireman was the lowly son of a **NORMANTON** farmer. He began his working life by selling flat irons in a London shop but soon set up in business on his own account, selling his pony for £15 and buying his own flat irons! He next leased an ironworks in Merthyr Tydfil and transformed the village from a hamlet to a great industrial centre in a few years. Using the latest technology – he was the first ironmaster to use the puddling process - he increased production from 10 tons per week in 1787 to over 200 tons by the time of his death in 1799. Crawshay and his dynasty inspired the iron making revolution in South Wales and the family became vastly rich, living in palatial splendour at Cyfarthfa Castle near the foundry. 'It is preserved in the tradition of the family,' said an ancestor, 'that when the 'Iron King' used to drive from his home in his coach-and-four into Wales, all the country turned out to see him, and quite a commotion took place when he passed through Bristol on his way to the works.'

CREWE, MRS

A curious article in the *Gentleman's Magazine* for 1753 about this **PONTEFRACT** alderman's wife, reveals an amusing fact about the estates of her late grandfather and a curious gift to that gentleman by a grateful King Charles II who wished to reward the loyalty shown by the family to his own father. The king was rather short of the jingling stuff so he conferred on the gentleman three baronetcies leaving the names of the recipients on the necessary paperwork blank so the honours could be sold on.

CRIGGLESTONE

A large parish formerly dominated by its colliery and coke ovens. In 1968, the character of the village was transformed by the construction of the M1 Motorway, investors taking advantage of the strategic location at Junction 29 to create new businesses including a mail order company.

CROFTON

Village between Wakefield and **NOSTELL**. It has an interesting church which, it is said, was built by Bishop Fleming of Lincoln who was born in

Crofton and died in 1431 (there is the sculpted motif of the bust of a bishop inside the church) and is home to a thriving **BRASS BAND**. Crofton Hall School, a private boarding establishment for girls, was once noted for its harsh regime. Fifteen-year-old Elizabeth Frith, a close friend of the Bronte sisters, kept a diary there in 1812: 'Several girls were sent to bed for losing at spelling. Miss Bitton had her dirty clothes pinned to her back for having them under the bed. Mary Wilson had the cap on for losing a French book and for cutting holes in her stockings. Mary Wilson was whipped for raising a report about Miss Fayre.' In 1920, the village was the scene of the gruesome and public murder of a local girl called Jane **DARWELL**.

CROMEK, THOMAS HARTLEY
Born in 1809, this vibrant and spectacular landscape and topographical watercolourist developed a highly individual style. On a grand tour of Europe from 1831 until 1839, he painted classical subjects in Italy, Greece, Belgium, Germany, Switzerland and Constantinople. For a time, he lived in Wakefield, *White's Directory* for 1853 recording his residency at an address in Hatfield Road. His paintings were very popular with the aristocracy, purchasers including Queen Victoria and the Earl of Harewood. He died in 1873. The artist's pictures can be seen in the British Museum and in the Fitzwilliam Gallery.

CROOK, GEORGE
Founder of a prominent firm of local builders who made a significant contribution to the civic and urban fabric of Wakefield and its district over fifty years in the first quarter of the twentieth century. The firm erected properties in Lincoln Street and, between 1901 and 1903, built terraces in Whitehall Street, Dewsbury Road also working on **WAKEFIELD PRISON**. Crook bought out the Westgate Brick Company in 1907. In 1908, his company erected the Police Headquarters in **WOOD STREET, WAKEFIELD**, his other prestigious projects including the Empire Theatre, an extension to **WAKEFIELD COUNTY HALL**, Snapethorpe and Manygates Schools and Snapethorpe Hospital together with local authority housing estates at Lupset, Peacock and Portobello estates. As a testament to the company's skill and expertise, it was awarded a contract for vital restoration work at **WAKEFIELD CATHEDRAL** in 1933. Supervising stonemason William Thickett specified stone from the **NEWMILLERDAM** quarry for the work, the quarry having to be re-opened to provide the necessary material.

CROWTHER, DOCTOR CALEB
Prominent Wakefield medical doctor and Non-Conformist who founded almshouses in Almshouse Lane. These were designed by a fellow worshipper – railway contractor William **SHAW**. Caleb stipulated that his

establishment's trustees should not be Roman Catholics or solicitors. And they all had to agree in writing not to become members of the Church of England or to vote Tory! Crowther was a GP in Wakefield and senior physician at the **WEST RIDING PAUPER LUNATIC ASYLUM**, regarding himself as an authority on mental illness.

CUSSONS, J W
Post office and chemist shop proprietor who ran his business in **OSSETT** between 1895 and 1900. He went on to produce the famous Imperial Leather Soap, which still sells in huge quantities throughout the world. Cussons carved monogram survives on the Prospect Road façade of his former premises.

D

DANDO, TOM
When this popular and able **ACKWORTH** councillor died in 1982, he was remembered in the creation of a country footpath known as The Dando Way. The route utilises the former track of the Brackenhill Light Railway, which was used until the 1950s to transport coal from the colliery at **HEMSWORTH**.

DARRINGTON
Ancient village strategically placed on the line of the **GREAT NORTH ROAD**. In the coaching era, its inns entertained hundred of coaches every day. It has a venerable Saxon church, one of the top 100 listed buildings in England and a ruined windmill, which preserves some of its machinery. Lady Kathleen **PILKINGTON** ran a fifty-bed hospital for injured First World War soldiers in Darrington Hall. It closed in 1919 having treated 406 patients. The village suffered a major catastrophe in September 1943 when a Halifax Bomber crashed, demolishing properties on the main road and in Chapel Hill. Four members of the Dean family were killed, three daughters having narrow escapes. Six crew members in the stricken aircraft also died. Enemy **AIR RAIDS** on Wakefield were numerically less fatal, the RAF ironically killing more people in the district than the Luftwaffe.

DARWELL, JANE
This nineteen-year-old bar maid at the *Royal Oak* in **CROFTON** had an amorous, but short-lived relationship with local miner Edwin Sowerby in 1920. After a few weeks, her ardour cooled and she ended her involvement. Much distressed, her twenty-eight year old former boyfriend fell into a black

despair and during a local cricket club dance around midnight on 26 October, he invaded the dance floor and slashed Jane across the throat with a razor, killing her instantly. He then tried to cut his own throat but he was stopped and arrested. Found guilty of murder, he was hanged by Albert Pierrepoint in Armley Gaol, Leeds. Pierrepoint went on to execute '**LORD HAW HAW**' and John George **HAIGH**. It was reported that Sowerby went to the gallows clutching a photograph of the murdered girl.

DENNINGTON SPA

Small hamlet in the parish of **CRIGGLESTONE** once renown for its medicinal spring.

DOG WHIPPERS

Dog Whippers and Sluggard Wakers were once employed in Wakefield Parish Church (now the cathedral) for dealing with stray canines and members of the congregation who fell asleep during sermons. Sometimes, one person performed both duties. Stray dogs were whipped from the church before services began, the eagle-eyed 'jobsworth' then taking his station at the back of the congregation to watch for sluggards. Any worshipper who nodded off would be rudely roused with a wand or a long staff. Wands were forked at the end. The fork would be pushed round the neck of the sleeper and given a good shake. Staffs were sometimes fitted at both ends to cope with the snorings of either sex. A fox's brush would be tickled into the faces of sleeping females. Men would receive a stout tap from a brass knob. The Wakefield Churchwardens Accounts for 1616 show that a man called Gorly Stork was paid 2 shillings and 6 pence for 'whippinge doggs'. Mr Lyght Owler received 1 shilling and 4 pence for a similar service in 1625 and 1628.

DOLPHIN

Public house at the corner of Warrengate and Kirkgate, Wakefield, once popular across Yorkshire for its striptease shows.

DOM PEDRO II

Emperor of Brazil who on 7 August 1871 visited **NORMANTON** with his Empress. Travelling by special train from York, they came to discuss the profit sharing scheme at **WHITWOOD COLLIERY**. In the emperor's honour, the newly sunk shaft at the Good Hope Pit at Loscoe was named after him, the mine subsequently becoming known, with a slight deviation in spelling, as the Don Pedro Colliery. During his visit, the emperor also inspected **NORMANTON FORGE**, ordering 10,000 miles of its celebrated steel-top rails for his railway in Brazil.

DONNER, IZAAK

The joint founder of the Wakefield Shirt Company came to England to escape Jewish persecution in 1939 and, encouraged by the warm welcome he received in Wakefield, set up a shirt manufacturing company with partner Frank Myers in Kirkgate. Here, he manufactured the famous Double Two shirts – the provision of a second collar proving a hit with men worldwide. He also produced the world's first Terylene shirt. His company prospered and in 1952, production was switched to Portobello Mills on Thornes Lane Wharf, the factory employing 500 people. An industrious and popular family man, he died at the helm of his company in 2000.

DRAKE AND WATERS

Prominent firm of shop-fitters situated in New Wells, Wakefield. Founded in 1924, the company secured a government contract to build seventy-two World War Two landing assault craft for invasion forces. These were constructed from mahogany using teenage girl labour. The craft were launched into the **CALDER RIVER** from a special slipway. During the war, the firm helped repair bomb damage in Sheffield.

DRAKE, FRANCIS

Born in **HEMSWORTH** in 1696, he was the son of the local rector. He left for York in 1717 and became a successful surgeon, his appointment as City Surgeon in 1727 allowing him to indulge his passion for history. He became a distinguished historian and antiquary; his most famous and long enduring work *Eboracum – The History and Antiquities of York* appearing in 1736 to great acclaim. Drake died in 1771.

Francis Drake. Extract fr
Old Yorkshire, edited by
William Smith, 1884.

DRAKE, NATHAN

Chronicler who came to live with his wife in **PONTEFRACT** and wrote contemporary, blow-by-blow diary accounts of the siege of **PONTEFRACT CASTLE** in 1648.

Feb 18th - being Shrove Tuesday – the besieged shot two pieces of cannon into the sentry houses at the lower end of Northgate which was then set on fire by the besiegers and one cannon into the Market Place and the besieged killed that day five men out of the round tower into the works from the ward houses along the ditch with musket shot.

Feb 26th – the besieged shot three cannon into the Market Place and 1 cannon to the besiegers guns where many of the besiegers men were killed and that day there was killed Captain Maullett on top of the round tower, being shot into the head with a musket bullet. (The grammar and spelling of these graphic entries has been modernised)

DRIFFIELD, LESLIE

A resident of Hundill Hall, East Hardwick, Driffield was an exceptionally talented billiard's player who dominated the game for many years. He won the Amateur Championships eight times in 1952, 1953, 1954, 1957, 1958, 1959, 1962 and 1967 and became World Professional Billiards Champion in 1971 and 1973 respectively beating Jack Karnehm and Albert Johnson. He was an incurable addict of billiards and could be found almost every morning of the year on the doorstep of the famous Smith and Nelson Snooker Hall in Leeds waiting for the doors to open. The player hated defeat. 'I have never seen anyone so eager to score and keep on scoring' commented one spectator. 'I have seen Driffield in matches with such a lead that he could not possibly lose and yet he would still double-baulk his opponent.'

DROVERS

Over the centuries millions of Scottish cattle were driven through the district on the way to southern markets, whole herds travelling along the **GREAT NORTH ROAD**. Drovers would rest in **WENTBRIDGE** half way between Edinburgh and London, the former *Bay Horse* inn near the bridge providing accommodation for the men and pasturage for up to 700 beasts. The inn had a forge to allow each animal to be re-shod. Calves could not keep pace with the adult animals and had to be lashed to carts.

DUNDERDALE, DAVID

Manufacturer of pottery in **CASTLEFORD** from 1790 until 1820. A Leeds linen merchant, he inherited the brick, tile and coarse pottery business from his father and produced new, more sophisticated wares inspired by the Leeds Pottery and the designs of Wedgewood. The factory was noted for its cream ware and uncoloured black basalt and white porcelain tea sets decorated with ornaments in relief. Many pieces were exported to the United States and continental Europe. The Napoleonic blockade of 1806 virtually stopped the export trade and Dunderdale had to sell his home – Dunford House – to keep his business afloat. But it foundered and went into liquidation. Surviving pieces from the Castleford Pottery fetch high prices. Its 1796 pattern book is still in existence.

DUNHILL, GEORGE

Pontefract chemist who first manufactured liquorice confectionery commercially in 1760. He added sugar to an ancient recipe developed by the local **CLUNIAC MONKS** to produce the famous **PONTEFRACT CAKES or YORKSHIRE PENNIES**.

DUNLOP SLAZENGER

International sports equipment company resident in the Wakefield District for 140 years and now based at the **WAKEFIELD 41 INDUSTRIAL ESTATE**.

DUPIER, SOLOMON

Wealthy resident of **PONTEFRACT** who died in 1732, his will providing money for the erection of **PONTEFRACT BUTTERCROSS** in 1734. A member of the garrison of Gibraltar easily assaulted by an Anglo-Dutch force in 1704, he cooperated with Admiral Sir George Rooke in ceding the Rock into British hands, receiving a pension for his services. He lived in some style in his adopted town and gave silver plate to the church in **DARRINGTON** where he is buried.

E

EAST HARDWICK

Sought after residential village and former agricultural centre, the home of Stephen **CAWOOD** and the famous author, poet and historian **J S FLETCHER**. Hardwick Hall was demolished in 1960 but several other buildings including a Queen Anne cottage and a roofed medicinal well survive.

EFFIGIES

Life-size church monuments in stone or materials such as alabaster depicting deceased persons of noble or eminent rank. They are often depicted in ecclesiastical or military mode, offering great insights into period dress and accoutrements. Effigies were expensive works of art and were the preserve of the influential and wealthy. In times of conflict, they attracted acts of desecration and vandalism. The circa 1325 effigy of Sir Warin de Scargill in the chancel of the church in **DARRINGTON**, is typically defaced, having lost its hands and having suffered mutilation to the forearms.

The mutilated effigy of Sir Warin de Scargill in Darrington Church.
LMA

ELEPHANT AND CASTLE

Attractive Wakefield public house with a colourful tiled façade on the **WESTGATE RUN**. The pub suffered an arson attack in December 1999, the fire destroying a collection of heritage photographs of the licensed trade in the city. Earlier, it was used during the 1800s for public **FLOGGINGS**.

EMLEY

Largely rural hill top village dominated by one of the tallest structures in Europe. A popular residential area, it was much favoured by factory and colliery owners, three colliery proprietors by the name of Jagger residing there in 1822. The village has its own **BRASS BAND**.

EMLEY MOOR TELEVISION MAST

Dominating concrete structure that commands the skyline above **EMLEY** village. The original mast which entered service in 1956 was replaced ten years later by a 1000 feet plus monster - the tallest in Europe. This mast catastrophically collapsed after adverse weather in March 1969, a subsequent investigation citing design-fault oscillations as the primary cause. Against the wishes of local residents who feared for their safety, a replacement was erected using a new design in flexing concrete, this mark-three self-supporting TV mast rising to a UK record-breaking height of 1083 feet.

EMPIRE STORES

One of the UK's largest mail order companies. The firm can trace its origins to a travelling pedlar who took to the road in 1820. Established as Fattorini & Sons in Bradford, the company opened a warehouse in **HORBURY** in 1962. By 1965, there were 1500 employees. Further premises were opened in **CRIGGLESTONE** in 1974. In the 1970s, profits were hit by losses arising from the **GREAT TRAIN ROBBERY**.

ENGLAND'S

Long-remembered, long-established general furnishing and ironmongery emporium in **PONTEFRACT** Market Place. The firm produced its own branded bicycle called the Pomfret. During the Great War, a Canadian soldier found a seventeenth century **TRADE TOKEN** in Flanders with the legend 'ANN ENGLAND PONTEFRACT' on one side and the impression of an agricultural implement on the other.

F

FALCON AND FETTERLOCK

Devices on the standard of the Duke of York, who rode out from his stronghold at **SANDAL CASTLE** in 1460 to death and defeat at the Battle of **WAKEFIELD GREEN**.

FEATHERSTONE

A proud and much improved former colliery village, home to a famous rugby club. The ancient All Saints' Church has a peal of bells dated 1146. A prominent local manor house was demolished in the 1950s. To commemorate the centenary of the infamous massacre, a distinctive sculpture was erected in the shopping precinct in 1993.

FEATHERSTONE MASSACRE

Violence perpetrated against miners who on 7 September 1893 demonstrated against a lock-out at Ackton Colliery. The miners were asked to disperse by armed government troops but they famously responded 'We would rather be shot through than hunger to death.' Eighteen of their number were hit by a hail of bullets, two men later dying of their wounds. A sculpture marks the site of the atrocity. Arthur **SCARGILL** is the author of a book about the event.

FEATHERSTONE ROVERS RUGBY FOOTBALL CLUB

Formed in 1902 and supported by the smallest population of any rugby league town, the club has achieved a host of honours including the Division I Championship in 1976/77 and Challenge Cup wins in 1966/67, 1972/73 and 1982/83. In their first Challenge Cup victory, with only limited funds but an unquenchable spirit, they saw off rivals Wakefield and triumphed 8-7 over Castleford before an all-ticket capacity crowd of 15,000. Leeds were dispatched in the semi-final and Barrow were beaten at Wembley, the press noting the feat with the acknowledgement: 'For a spirit like this can never be bought.' Famous international players in the roll-of-honour include Tommy Askin, Don Fox, Jim Thompson, Deryck Fox and home-grown Paul Newlove who became the world's most valuable player.

FERRY BOAT INN, STANLEY

Imaginative waterside conversion inspired by Stanley Ferry's mercantile past. The inn has an attractive **TOM PUDDING** restaurant.

FERRYBRIDGE

Important former coaching stop on the line of the **GREAT NORTH ROAD** readily identified today by its massive power station and cooling towers and the thunderous A1. The coaching era lasted from 1786 until the 1840s. Half way between London and Edinburgh, the town was ideally placed to cater for the travelling classes. It had three major inns – *The Angel, The Golden Lion* and

The Greyhound - an inn that catered for stage wagons and a custom house. It is thought that Sir Walter Scott wrote part of his novel *Heart of Midlothian* while staying at a Ferrybridge inn on his way north to Scotland. The town is also famous for its pottery established in 1793.

FIELDING, HELEN
Author born in Morley near Leeds in 1958. Fielding attended **WAKEFIELD GIRLS' HIGH SCHOOL** before studying English at Oxford. Her second novel, *Bridget Jones Diary* detailing the shallow and superficial life of a single woman was a worldwide success. It was adapted for a popular film of the same name.

FIRE ENGINE
The first recorded use of a device for extinguishing fires in Wakefield was in 1778, a horse-drawn machine attending a blaze at Mr Smith's dye house in Thornes Lane.

FIVE TOWNS RESOURCE AND TECHNOLOGY CENTRE
Educational and training enterprise established in Welbeck Street, **CASTLEFORD** offering services for local unemployed, unwaged and part-time workers.

FLANSHAW
Once an intensive agricultural centre noted for its dairies and market gardens. Oakes Mill, renamed Moorhouses Mill produced woollens, Talbot's Confectionery Works supplying humbugs, mint imperials, toffees and Yorkshire mixtures until its closure around 1960. The imposing Sirdar factory (formerly Harrap Brothers) currently dominates the employment scene manufacturing knitting wools for home and international markets.

FLETCHER J S
A prolific journalist, author, poet and historian with more than 280 books to his credit. He lived in Cawood House, **EAST HARDWICK** and wrote *When Charles I Was King* (set in **DARRINGTON**) and numerous detective novels with titles such as *Murder of the Ninth Baronet*, *Three Day's Terror* and *The Mazaroff Murder*. As a journalist, he was a popular writer under the banner 'Son of the Soil' for the *Leeds Mercury*. His books were very popular in the United States – the President Woodrow Wilson read *The Middle Temple Murder* while recuperating in hospital - but were never fully appreciated in his native Yorkshire, the county inspiring *Daniel Quayne* and *The Threshing Floor*. Was this partly because he gave **PONTEFRACT** and its worthies (to quote his own son) such a 'terrible roasting' in his book *The Town of Crooked Ways*?

His studies, *Making of Modern Yorkshire* and *Memorials of a Yorkshire Parish* are regarded as the most valuable of his works.

FLOGGINGS

Corporal punishment inflicted in the eighteenth and nineteenth centuries. In Wakefield, floggings took place in the yard of the **ELEPHANT AND CASTLE** public house in Westgate. One eyewitness describes the process thus: 'I have a vivid memory of seeing public floggings take place in the streets of Wakefield, the 'Cat' being at that time freely administered for comparatively slight offences. The flogging generally used to begin at twelve o'clock...our benevolent schoolmaster used to let us out a quarter of an hour early in order that we might not miss the spectacle. The wretched culprit was tied with outstretched arms to the back of a cart which was drawn at a tolerable foot's pace. The whip used was a formidable weapon, having nine strings of whip-cord about two feet in length with a knot tied on each string at intervals of two inches.' The prescribed number of lashes was delivered by a powerful prisoner officer on the bare back of the criminal with gusto. When the flogging ceased, the bloody wounds were bathed in a mixture of gunpowder and water. The barbaric practice is thought to have ceased around 1814.

FOTHERGILL, DOCTOR JOHN

Swaledale doctor and social pioneer who campaigned against the slave trade. He was an advocate of prison reform and the benefits of vaccination against smallpox and he lobbied for the end of the American War of Independence. He helped set up several medical schools in the United States and he founded **ACKWORTH SCHOOL**. Throughout his life, the doctor gave large sums of money to good causes, dying with only a modest estate.

FRENCH NUNS

Displaced by the consequences of the French Revolution, a party of nuns belonging to the Benedictine sisterhood fled to England. They were initially welcomed in London by the Catholic wife of the Prince Regent (later George IV) who provided them with temporary accommodation. After a time, they came to Yorkshire and lived between 1811 and 1821 in **HEATH OLD HALL** where, far from home, they all eventually died. They are buried in almost anonymous graves in St Peter's churchyard in **KIRKTHORPE**. Nearly all have gravestones marked with initials and the date of death although one stone has the following inscription: 'Emilia Monteiro. Born at Lisbon. Died July 3rd 1816.'

FRICKLEY COLLIERY

A major employer in **SOUTH ELMSALL**, the pit was sunk in 1903. In 1925 an adjacent power station was built to supply electricity to the mine,

An early view of Frickley Colliery. Brian Elliott Collection

excess production augmenting the National Grid and supplying some local villages and other mines in the area. The pit was profitably worked almost to the end of its life in 1993.

FROBISHER, SIR MARTIN

Born around 1535 in Altofts, **NORMANTON**, this Elizabethan explorer began his naval career as a privateer but his remarkable seamanship and navigation skills were recognised by the queen who personally sponsored three of his expeditions, one of them to Hudson Bay. In 1588, he achieved immortality in helping to repulse the Armada, one account of his exploits recording: 'He had the prudence of Hawkins with the resolution and quickness of Drake, while his dauntless courage was all his own. It was valour spiced with what can only be described as devilry, acquired in his privateering days. His seamanship has perhaps never been surpassed.' Frobisher lived in the long demolished three-storey Frobisher Hall in

Stained glass window in All Saints' Church, Normanton. LMA

Altofts. A memorial window in All Saints' Church in Normanton draws visitors from as far away as Frobisher Bay in Canada.

FRYSTON COLLIERY

Opened in 1896, the pit recruited local men, miners also coming from the Durham and Staffordshire coalfields. One of the most colourful managers in its history was a man called Fisher. A former miner recalled his aggressive and callous manner. " 'I was 14 when I got my arm fast in a pulley. It was a right mess; covered in blood. 'Where do you think you're going with him?' asked Fisher. 'He's injured; he's going home,' answered my workmates. Fisher scowled. 'We can't lose coal because of him. Give him a job where he needs only one arm!' " Another miner shivered at his own memories. 'I started at Fryston in 1928. I was fourteen. Up at half three, walk to pit, back home turned four in the afternoon and all for two bob a day and a clip round the ear if you weren't working.' A miner's wife recalled some happier days. 'In many ways, my husband never really left the pit. He draws and paints his memories of life at Fryston, the laughs and the sadness. He had an exhibition of his artwork at the Royal Festival Hall in London. He felt so proud he did. His mates must have been proud too. After all, it was entirely based on his loving memories of his working life with them.' The lady was referring to Harry **MALKIN**. Before the pit closed in 1985, much of its production was delivered by barge to the nearby CEGB power stations.

G

GARDE IMPERIALE

Re-enactment association set up in 1972 by a Bonapartist descendent of a French prisoner-of-war who was captured after the Battle of Waterloo in 1815 and sent to Wakefield. With other enthusiasts, including several recruits from Wakefield, he formed a Yorkshire cohort of old soldiers to recreate the dress and drill of Napoleon's Old Guard. This splendid body of men has marched through Paris.

GARFORTH, SIR WILLIAM EDWARD

Pioneering mining engineer and JP who first came to Yorkshire in 1879 as agent for Pope and Pearson's Colliery in **ALTOFTS**. He devised washing and screening processes to reduce the risk of coal dust explosions and organised the rescue of miners at his own pit 'one of the best managed collieries in England' following a disaster on 2 October 1886. Twenty-one men and fifty-three horses died in the tragedy, Garforth deploying his own Rescue Corps with great personal leadership and bravery. His subsequent publication *Rules for Recovering Coal Mines After Explosions and Fires* became a standard text book. Garforth went on to develop equipment and techniques for saving life and perfected a gas testing and breathing apparatus dubbed the 'Weg' after his own initials. He also perfected a Deep Undercut Coal Cutting Machine. He was elected President of the Institute of Mining Engineers and given a knighthood in 1914.

GASKELL, DANIEL

Wakefield's first MP and well-known and respected owner of Lupset Hall for almost seventy-five years. He was a generous benefactor to educational and religious establishments throughout the district, his home presenting 'an ever open door to pilgrims and strangers of distinction from all lands. Thither came politicians, philanthropists, social reformers, Polish and Hungarian refuges, Hindoo Pundits and distinguished dramatists, to say nothing of literary men and women of all degrees of fame and graduations of gifts.' Gaskell is buried in the catacombs of **WAKEFIELD, WESTGATE CHAPEL**.

GAWTHORPE

Famous for originating and hosting the **WORLD COAL CARRYING CHAMPIONSHIPS**. The village has its own **BRASS BAND**.

GEORGE-A-GREEN

The pinder of Wakefield, who, in legend, was a rival of Robin **HOOD**. He excelled at running, archery, leaping and wresting. Beatrice, the pinder's lady and the daughter of Justice Grymes – she was known as 'the flower of the north' – was said to be as equally as attractive as Maid Marion. 'This George-A-Green was the famous Pinder of Wakefield, who fought with Robin Hood and Little John both together, and got the better of them, as the old ballad tells us. Called George-A-Green because he wore a green bay in his hat.'

GISSING CENTRE

Small museum dedicated to the works of novelist George **GISSING**. Located in the author's former childhood home at 2-4 Thompson's Yard off Westgate, the museum (open Saturdays from May to September) has copies of his works and associated memorabilia. Gissing described the view from his home in *A Life's Morning*: 'The uppermost windows commanded a view of the extensive cattle market, of a long railway viaduct and hilly fields beyond.' Another home reference can be found in his *Reminiscences of my Father*: 'I was oil-painting in the little spare bedroom which I used as a studio (looking out into Thompson's Yard) one day in 1870 when father came in to tell me that the Franco – Prussian war had begun.'

GISSING, GEORGE

Talented but ill-starred gothic-genre novelist born in Wakefield in 1857. George Orwell once described him as '...perhaps the best novelist England has produced.' The brilliant son of a local chemist, he was despatched, at the age of thirteen, to an Alderley Edge boarding school. He won a scholarship to Owens College Manchester (later Manchester University) two years later and seemed destined for a bright literary future. But, motivated by his infatuation for a prostitute, he stole money from the students' cloakroom and was imprisoned for a month. He married the prostitute who died from syphilis in 1888. In that year, his book *A Life's Morning* was serialised in *The Cornhill Magazine*, the book making many references to Wakefield and is people. He also described the environs of Stoneleigh Terrace on Doncaster Road, his mother relocating there after the death of her husband in 1870. A second marriage proved equally disastrous, his dark moods, exacerbated by his experiences amongst the down-and-outs of London, spawning a series of depressing but visceral so-called 'slum novels' beginning with the *Workers* and ending with the reasonably successful *The Nether World*. Newly appreciated in recent years, his undoubted masterpiece is *New Grub Street*. Gissing sold the copyright in this works outright and never received the financial reward due his genius. He died poor and disillusioned at the age of 46 in France in 1903. The author's boyhood home is now the **GISSING CENTRE**. In total, the author wrote twenty-three novels, two studies of Charles Dickens, a travel book and numerous short stories. His ambitions to write a history of Wakefield between 1850 and 1870 were never fulfilled.

George Gissing, 1857-1903 and the family home (bay window).
Courtesy of the Gissing Trust

GISSING, MARGARET AND ELLEN

Members of the famous literary family, the sisters jointly ran a private boys' preparatory school in Cliff Hill House, Sandy Walk, Wakefield from 1906. The small school had two classrooms where both sisters taught. One former pupil recalled being despatched into the town before lessons began to buy treacle from Moorhouse's shop in Northgate and tapers from the Webster's store in Westgate.

GISSING, THOMAS, WALLER

Father of the famous author who moved to Wakefield in 1856 to run a chemists shop in Westgate. A talented apothecary, amateur botanist and poet with a bent for science, he joined the Mechanics' Institution and became its librarian in 1868. He quickly integrated himself into the cultural and political life of the city and became a Liberal Member of the City Council in 1867. He studied the botany of the district in his spare time and gathered specimens for use in his botanical preparations. His *Ferns of Wakefield and Neighbourhood* appeared in 1862, *Materials for a Flora of Wakefield* following in 1867. The author had three sons and two daughters Margaret and Ellen, a book of remembrances by Doctor Henry Hick revealing that 'the whole family was always grubbing in hedge bottoms.' Thomas Gissing died in 1870 at the early age of 41, a eulogy by his council colleagues emphasising the exceptional impact he made on the district in just fourteen years.

GLASSHOUGHTON BUSINESS, LEISURE AND RETAIL PARK

Transformed from a wasteland blighted by the dereliction of a former colliery and a coking works near **CASTLEFORD**, this integrated development at Junction 32 of the M62 accommodates housing, small warehouses and office units, the Freeport Factory Outlet and **XSCAPE**.

GODBER, JOHN

Born into a mining family at **UPTON** in 1956, this prolific playwright is one of the most performed writers in the English language. He studied at Minsthorpe High School returning there as Head of Drama after training at **BRETTON HALL UNIVERSITY COLLEGE**. In 1984 he was appointed Artistic Director of the Hull Truck Theatre Company. His many internationally popular works include *Bouncers* based on his experiences of Wakefield nightlife at Kiko's nightspot in **PONTEFRACT**, *Up'n'Under* inspired by rugby league, *On The Piste* and *April In Paris*.

GOLDEN COCK INN

One of Wakefield's long-lost architectural gems, this richly carved and jettied seventeenth century structure in Little Westgate was demolished in 1963.

GOLD FEVER

In 1825 an attractive prospectus was issued by the Anglo-Chilean Mining Association, offering shares in a lucrative venture to extract gold, silver, copper and tin from mines in South America. Local lawyer Twistleton Haxby was part of a legal partnership set up in 1811 with David Colvard - his name in the firms promotional literature was swaggeringly suffixed with the words 'Honest – What About The Rest?' Haxby was attracted by the prospect of easy money and invested £2000. He never saw a return. He lost his shirt and normally canny Yorkshire folk should have learnt from his mistake. But the speculative serpent raised its glittering head again twenty-six years later when in 1851, shares in the Anglo-Californian Gold Mining Company were offered for sale. Several Wakefield investors were smitten with gold fever including a butcher's widow from Wild's Yard, Kirkgate, two travelling salesman and a George Street grocer. They would have found more gold in their teeth.

GOODCHILD, JOHN

A passionate archivist, antiquarian and local historian with hundreds of published books and pamphlets to his credit. Mr Goodchild runs an independent local history study centre in Wakefield covering the central 'West Riding'. Developed over fifty years, his unique million-strong collection embraces manuscripts, books, maps and illustrations and is available for research purposes by appointment free of charge. His eclectic treasury also includes such artefacts as Roman coins, a length of line from Smithson's Railway at Low Laithes and butter pats used at Armitage's grocery shop in **OSSETT**.

John Goodchild at his desk. LMA

GOURANGA

Exclamatory word inciting happiness scribbled and scrawled on urban pavements and walls and on motorway bridges in Wakefield District and elsewhere by unknown graffitists.

GRAFT

A euphemistic local term for physical endeavour usually uttered in the same sentence as 'never buy owt wi' a wooden handle …it allus means hard work.'

GREAT NORTH ROAD

Historically, England's principal north-south road access (the modern A1) built partly on the line of the Roman's Ermine Way, which linked London and Winteringham on the south bank of the Humber during the Julio-Claudian period.

GREAT TRAIN ROBBERY

Systematic and highly organised theft of **EMPIRE STORES** mail order parcels during the early 1970s from unlocked railway wagons kept overnight at Wakefield goods yard. Management became increasingly suspicious when thousands of despatched goods failed to reach their destinations, 951 parcels disappearing in one month alone. The police were called in and fifty suspects were interviewed, home searches revealing stashed treasure troves of purloined goods. Twenty-five people were charged with theft and nine were given custodial sentences. The court heard that the thefts had the 'added thrill of a perpetual Christmas, as it was never known what was in the next mailbag.' The magnitude of the thefts was never properly calculated but the firm estimated that at least 500 mailbags containing 7000 orders went missing.

GREAVES, JOHN

A distinguished freemason who was elected to the St Oswald Lodge in **PONTEFRACT** in 1889, Greaves was a gentle giant of a man, generally believed to have been around 7 feet 3 inches tall. He was 'proportionate in body and limb and stoutness' but displayed, like many tall men, a gentleness and humility that brought him many friends. He died in 1893.

GREEN, EDWARD

A Wakefield inventor born in 1799, Green – known as 'Old Neddy' to his workforce - took over a local foundry in Ings Road and manufactured wrought ironwork and steam machinery. Inspired by the work of James Watt, he patented his 'Green's Economiser', a device that utilised waste steam to pre-heat boiler tanks and reduce the consumption of coal. His system was a worldwide success although it was regarded with some trepidation by local mine owners who thought it might reduce the demand for fuel! Business boomed and in 1851, his invention was exhibited at the Great Exhibition. His firm moved to Calder Vale Road. Prominent in local affairs and a real benefactor to his home town, Green died in 1865. The improved but fundamentally unchanged 'Green's Economiser' is still in use today. Green's son Edward – 'Young Neddy' - leased **HEATH OLD HALL** after his father's death and was elected to Parliament as MP for Wakefield in 1885. He was rewarded with a baronetcy in the following year but criticised in Ruskin's periodical *Fors Clavigera* for industrialising Wakefield. His elder son Lycett was involved in the Royal Baccarat Scandal of 1890. His younger son Frank lived in palatial style in York's Treasurer's House between 1897 and 1914. In 1912, King George V visited the Wakefield factory and innocently asked Lycett what benefits had accrued from 'Old Neddy's' invention. 'Foxhunting and champagne, your Majesty!' was the bold reply.

GREEN, JOE

This fifty-four-year-old miner from **KELLINGLEY COLLIERY** died on 15 June 1984 during a miners' **STRIKE**. He was on picket duty outside Ferrybridge Power Station when he was crushed and killed. His funeral at Pontefract Crematorium on 22 June was attended by 8000 supporters and was widely covered by the media. The sombre procession was accompanied by the strains of a lone Scottish piper who played a lament. The death helped to strength the miner's iron resolve. Fellow miner David Jones died in similar circumstances. The tragic deaths and linked events, inspired a song – *The Ballad of '84* by lyricist and composer Dick Gaughan who wrote:

> *Let's pause here to remember the men who gave their lives,*
> *Joe Green and David Jones were killed in fighting for their rights.*

The North Staffordshire Miners' Wives Action Group commissioned a sculpture in memory of the strike martyrs. This was made by Frank Casey and unveiled at the Potteries Museum in Stoke-on-Trent in 1991. In recent years, an annual Memorial Day event has been held in Barnsley.

GULLEY (OR GULLY) JOHN

This versatile and extremely busy gentleman was a butcher, a convict, a prizefighter, a prolific horseracing punter and a **PONTEFRACT** MP from 1832 to 1837 when he lived in **ACKWORTH** Park. His election to Parliament was celebrated in the following poem:

> *You ask me the cause that made Pontefract sully*
> *Her fame by returning to Parliament Gully?*
> *The etymological cause, I suppose, is –*
> *His breaking the bridges of so many noses.*

In a celebrated fight with Henry Pearce – 'The Game Chicken' - he was beaten after 64 rounds but he went on to become bare-knuckle champion, overcoming the giant Bob Gregson twice. He had considerable success in horse racing, winning the Derby and the St Leger in 1832, the Derby and Oaks in 1846, the Two Thousand Guineas in 1844 and the Derby and the Two Thousand Guineas in 1854. Somehow, he still found time to sire twenty-four children - twelve to each of two wives. He died in 1863 and is buried in **ACKWORTH** in land he bought specially for the purpose.

H

HAGENBACH, CHARLES
Well-known pre-war Wakefield baker and confectioner with shops in the city centre and outlets in **CASTLEFORD, PONTEFRACT, HORBURY** and **OSSETT**. The firm had its own distinctive fleet of delivery vans. Its main shop was on the corner of Northgate and Union Street. The bakehouse was up Old Crown Yard.

John Gulley. Pontefract Museum

HAIGH, JOHN, GEORGE
Serial killer born in 1910. He lived, as a child, on Ledger Lane in **OUTWOOD** and became a pupil at the **WAKEFIELD QUEEN ELIZABETH'S GRAMMAR SCHOOL**. His father, a member of the Plymouth Brethren, brought up his only child under strict rules, fencing off the garden to avoid contamination by the outside world. A Bible thumper who worked as a power station foreman, he had a forehead scar which he attributed to the Devil, dark references to retribution and avenging angels filling his son's mind with nightmare visions of bloodied crucifixes. The young man won a choral scholarship to attend the grammar school and frequently sang in the cathedral choir. A career criminal he went to London and began a murderous spree leading to six brutal slayings and two shivering epithets – the *Acid Bath Murderer* and the *Vampire Killer*. Haigh first shot his victims – they was some evidence that he drank their blood - and attempted to dispose of the bodies by dissolving them in sulphuric acid. He was convicted (one of his victim's dentures and a gall stone proved impervious to acid) and executed by fellow Yorkshireman Albert Pierrepoint at Wandsworth in 1949. Pierrepoint had previously executed **'LORD HAW HAW'** and

Edwin Sowerby, the murderer of Jane **DARWELL**. Haigh agreed to a death mask being made by Madame Tussauds and he donated his clothing to the wax works on the understanding that his trousers were always kep scrupulously pressed and his shirt cuffs clean. His effigy may be seen in the Chamber of Horrors to this day.

HALIFAX GIBBET
Upon conviction of the theft of two horses (together with the theft of sixteen yards of kersey) from a field in **SANDAL MAGNA**, A Mitchell and Wilkinson of Sowerby were both executed on the gibbet on 30 April 1650. A one time, the business-end of the gibbet was preserved in Wakefield.

HARK TO MOPSEY
Unusually named inn in **NORMANTON**. One explanation of the name supposes that around 1870, the landlord suffered regular ear-bashing from his garrulous wife Mopsey, sympathetic customers nodding during every onslaught with the comment: 'Hark to Mopsey'. Another suggests that the name derives from a foxhound puppy known as Mopsey, given to the landlord by the Earl Fitwilliam. Whenever the hunt passed the inn doors, the homesick dog would respond with a distinctive bark, the landlord acknowledging the intelligence of the animal with the words: 'Hark to Mopsey'. A third version supposes that the tearful landlord's wife, moping after the return of her pet to the pack, uttered the words whenever she heard the bell of her pet as it passed the door. Perhaps the most plausible source of the name, however, comes from the exceptional ability of the animal to sniff out foxes when the other dogs in the pack where ranging far and wide. Ignoring the rest of the frenzied baying, the master of the hunt would shout: 'Hark to Mopsey!'

HARRIS, JOANNE
Born in 1964, the daughter of a French mother and an English father, Harris spent the first three years of her life living with her parents and her paternal grandparents above the family sweet shop. She attended **WAKEFIELD GIRLS' HIGH SCHOOL** and became a teacher, latterly turning to literature and producing a string of popular novels including *Sleep Pale Sister Coastliners*, *Holy Fools*, *Blackberry Wine* and *Chocolat*. This title, inspired by the author's love of food and the exotic locale of the Loire, was adapted for a film of the same name.

HARRISON, JOHN
This lowly carpenter's son who was born in Foulby near **NOSTELL PRIORY** in 1693, took on the biggest scientific challenge of the day

inventing a marine chronometer that revolutionised navigation by allowing longitude to be fixed with great accuracy. It was described by Captain James Cook as '...our faithful guide through all the vicissitudes of climate'. But it was not all plain sailing, the achievement that sought to win a prize of an astonishing £20,000, requiring a lifetime of Yorkshire cussedness and determination. Harrison built three wonderfully engineered marine timekeepers with the prosaic nomenclatures H1, H2 and H3. None of the devices worked to the satisfaction of the adjudicating Board of Longitude. Undeterred, their maker went back to his workshop and produced a radically altered design, H4 undergoing sea trials in 1761. During its 43-day voyage, the chronometer lost 39.2 seconds and the

Plaque in Wragby. LMA

conditions of securing the prize were met. But it was not awarded, the board implying that the accuracy of H4 was a fluke. They were prepared to offer the inventor half the prize provided he fully disclosed all his design secrets and agreed to the testing of similar time-pieces. Harrison refused to comply. Eventually six experts examined H4 and agreed that it met every condition. But their lordships paid over only half the prize money and Harrison had to produce yet another chronometer - H5. And they were still not satisfied! The seventy-nine year old was outraged and he petitioned King George III to intervene. His highness met Harrison's son, allegedly remarking: '...these people have been cruelly wronged...' and 'by God Harrison, I will see you righted!' The king tested H5 himself and proved it to be wholly accurate but the Board of Longitude remained as implacable as ever. Finally, Harrison asked Parliament to settle the matter. Fully endorsing the supreme merits of the great man's work, MP's voted him £8,750 in June 1773. Harrison had finally won the prize, and with it, immortality. Three of

John Harrison clock at Nostell Priory.
John Goodchild Collection. Courtesy of
www.teixtaireandcalder.org.uk: The online archive
of Wakefield District Images

Harrison's early wooden clocks survive. One of these treasures may be seen in **NOSTELL PRIORY**. Harrison's more famous chronometers are in the National Maritime Museum in Greenwich.

HARRISON, MICHAEL

The captain of the England Rugby Union team between 1985 and 1987 Harrison was introduced to the game as a pupil in **WAKEFIELD QUEEN ELIZABETH'S GRAMMAR SCHOOL**.

HARTLEY, BERNARD AND JESSE

Famed architects and civil engineers from **CASTLEFORD**. The partnership produced **CASTLEFORD BRIDGE** and the river crossing at **FERRYBRIDGE** to a design by John **CARR**. Jesse Hartley designed the monumental Albert Docks in Liverpool.

HARTLEY, JOSHUA

This **CASTLEFORD** potter began his business around 1850, initially producing bricks, tiles, firebricks and chimney pots. His bricks were used in the construction of the housing estates in Ferry Fryston, Half Acres and **WHITWOOD**. Utilitarian production gave way to the manufacture of stoneware under the **HARTROX** brand.

HARTROX

Stamp or impressed provenance mark found on a variety of Joshua **HARTLEY** stoneware such as dishes, bowls and teapots. Sometimes used in association with the imprint of a stag.

HAWKE, LORD MARTIN BLADEN

Born in 1860 in Lincolnshire, this legendary Yorkshire cricketer – a real sport star who was profiled on a cigarette card of the period – studied at **PONTEFRACT KING'S SCHOOL**. Ironically, he enshrined the rule that only players born in the county could play for Yorkshire. He was associated with Yorkshire cricket for over fifty years – twenty-eight years as captain - and played in five Tests for England. A gentleman of the 'finest game in the world' he was a cricketing ambassador who toured widely and popularised the sport abroad. Lord Hawke was president of his Yorkshire club for forty years and president and treasurer of the MCC. He was a strict disciplinarian who controversially dropped star bowler Bobby Peel when the left-armer took the field drunk, the dismissal ending Peel's career. Lord Hawke pioneered the payment of winter allowances and he created his club's white rose symbol. When not playing cricket, he enjoyed foxhunting and became the Master of the **BADSWORTH HUNT**. He died in 1938.

HEATH HALL
A sumptuous house of 1754, with two storeys and eleven bays, designed by the celebrated John **CARR**.

HEATH OLD HALL
Built in the sixteenth century, a once beautiful multi-towered mansion on a cliff overlooking the **CALDER RIVER**. It was the home of Mary **BOLLES**, whose ghost haunted the hall and grounds. The hall was demolished in 1960 but one of its fireplaces with a date of 1584 was saved and preserved in the *Hazelwood Hall Hotel* near Tadcaster.

HEMSWORTH
Formerly a colliery village and the site of Holgate's Hospital founded by Robert **HOLGATE** the Archbishop of York in 1546 and rebuilt in the mid nineteenth century. When the owners of the colliery – it opened in 1876 - pressed for wage reductions in 1904 and 1905, miners withdrew their labour and they were evicted from their tied houses in **KINSLEY**. During another coal strike in 1919, sailors were brought in to maintain production. In 1960, unemployed Scottish miners were encourage to settle and work in the village and new accommodation – The Scotch Estate – was provided.

HEMSWORTH WATER PARK
A visionary but controversial colliery reclamation scheme sponsored by the local parish council and opened in 1987, the park provides a lake for integrated water sports including fishing. Pedaloes are available for hire, the facility providing the north's only inland beaches, a childrens' play park, a public house and a wildlife area.

HEPWORTH, BARBARA
Pioneering and versatile sculptor in ceramics, marble, bronze, and aluminium who was born in Wakefield in 1903. Her family home was at 15 Duke of York Street. She attended **WAKEFIELD GIRLS' HIGH SCHOOL,** Leeds School of Art and the Royal College of Art in London. In 1975 she was described

Barbara Hepworth.
Extract from Wakefield MDC's newsletter No 2.

by the *Guardian* as 'probably the most significant woman artist in the history of art to date.' Examples of her work can be seen in Castrop Rauxel Square opposite **COUNTY HALL** and in the garden of **WAKEFIELD ART GALLERY** as well as in galleries worldwide. Her work has inspired the creation of the **HEPWORTH GALLERY**.

HEPWORTH GALLERY
Imaginative art gallery - the iconic centrepiece of the **WAKEFIELD WATERFRONT** scheme - forming a new millennium arts centre to replace the existing facility in Wentworth Terrace by 2008. The gallery will display thirty original plaster sculptures by the artist together with finished examples of her work and a unique collection of tools and templates. The attraction will act as a catalyst for urban renaissance and should receive up to 141,000 visitors each year.

Mother and Child 1934 by Barbara Hepworth.
Extract from Wakefield MDC's newsletter No 2

Artist's impression of the Hepworth Gallery. Extract from Wakefield MDC's newsletter No 2

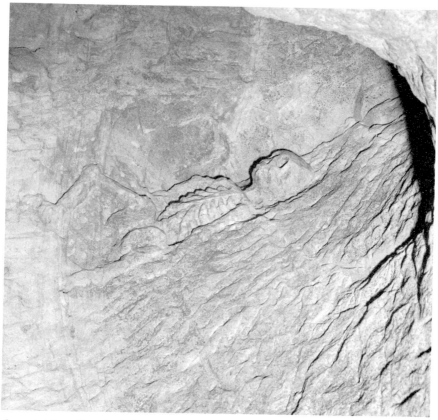

Carved skeleton figure in the Hermitage. LMA

HERMITAGE

A bizarre subterranean chapel located 15½ feet below the old dispensary in Southgate, **PONTEFRACT**. The fourteenth century excavation was rediscovered in 1854 by road workers who broke through a roof to reveal two dusty chambers, the reputed home of a hermit named Adam de Layerthorpe. His rent was 'one white rose to be paid at midsummer.' One successor troglodyte, John Queyks, sold papal indulgences from his lair. In 1213, one hermit, Peter of Pomfret, was hanged because he prophesied that King John would lose his throne.

HESSLE

This small hamlet north-west of **ACKWORTH** was mentioned in the Domesday Book and was once a thriving village on the main road between

Doncaster and Wakefield. It supported six ironsmiths – perhaps the largest concentration in the county – and was important for tanning and fellmongering. A highway realignment brought its modern isolation.

HERONRY AND WATERTON COUNTRYSIDE DISCOVERY CENTRE

Countryside attraction embracing woods, lakes, farmland and the former estate owned by Charles **WATERTON**. The nucleus of the area is the Anglers Country Park set around a trout-filled, wildfowl lake created from opencast mine workings.

HICKSON AND WELCH

Chemical works established in **CASTLEFORD** by London dye salesman Ernest Hickson in 1915. During the First World War, the firm manufactured tons of TNT for the military. In 1930, the factory exploded, killing thirteen people and injuring thirty-two more. There was widespread damage in the town – three hundred houses were made uninhabitable - and a subscription fund was set up to aid people made homeless. Local landowner and benefactor Ambrose **SHEPHERD** gave £50 to the fund. On 21 September 1992, another explosion at the plant killed five employees, a 300 feet fireball surging from the control room, across a car park and into a four-storey office block following the accidental ignition of a tank of nitrotoluene during routine maintenance work. 'Thank God it was lunchtime, otherwise I think we would have had more fatalities in the office block,' said an official press release. Today, the vast riverside plant produces a wide range of constituents for industry and the agrochemical and pharmaceutical sectors.

HIRST, FRED

Founder of the **WORLD COAL CARRYING CHAMPIONSHIPS** in **GAWTHORPE**. A local miner who worked at Lofthouse Colliery, he survived the war and a German POW camp to create the Guinness Book of Records event in 1963. He was a passionate supporter of the race and his village's annual maypole celebrations. He died in 2001.

HIRST SAMUEL

A well-to-do, hard-working farmer who ran Home Farm near Kellington from 1831 until his death at the age of seventy seven in 1880. Uniquely, he diligently kept a daily diary, never missing an entry until the last two weeks of his life when he dictated his words to a friend. The illuminating and sometimes highly amusing diary has survived, as the following extracts will show:

Tuesday 13th December 1831: At Ferrybridge. Rent Day. Got full of liquor-

very deep. Went to Pontefract Bank – took out a cheque for £200.

Tuesday 15th January 1833: I bled 11 beasts and gave them a drink each to stop them from casting their calves. Got two peacocks – a cock and a hen from Mr Hesletine of Barth House, Selby.

Friday 11th December 1835: Dr. Ibeson cut my throat 3 times now. He says I have a carbuncle in my throat. Got the bill. Rather strong £11.

Friday 21st February 1840: I knocked 4 teeth out of two horses mouths.

Wednesday 29th November 1859: Went before Pontefract Magistrate to swear to my coat stole from my room at the New Elephant Inn. Robert Bew of Selby is the prisoner.

Friday October 4th 1867: Bought two bricks of mushroom spawn – got mushroom house made. I have told the men we must lower the wages to 15 shillings.

Saturday 5th June 1869: Brought new carriage home today. Paid Atkinson for my tooth stuffing 2 shillings and 6 pence.

Friday 12th April 1872: Bought 6 dozen port 63 shillings – 6 dozen sherry 54 shillings and a case of champagne 74 shillings.

HOFFMAN'S PIES
Legendary crusted porcine delicacies produced since 1896 when the firm was established in a shop in Silver Street, Wakefield, the inspiration behind a local eulogy: 'I get's me gob round rim and sucks; then I twiddles me tongue and seeks to mek a 'ole in t'crust, sticking it in and letting the hot, sweet juices baptise me tonsils. Finally I get's me nashers round t'meeat and consummates job, burrowing me whole face in it as me body quivers wi ecstasy.'

HOLGATE, ARCHBISHOP ROBERT
Eminent divine born in **HEMSWORTH** in 1481. He was appointed to the relatively obscure bishopric of Llandaff in South Wales, afterwards becoming the Lord President of the Council of the North in 1538. Between 1545 and 1555, he became the first Protestant Archbishop of York and was the first of York's archbishops to marry. Following the death of Henry VIII and the accession of the Catholic Mary Tudor, he abandoned his religion and deserted his wife to avoid arrest. He retired to his birthplace and, in the year of his demise in 1555, founded a local hospital. In York, he endowed Archbishop Holgate's School. A suburb to the north-west of the city is named after him.

HOLMES, RICHARD
This celebrated nineteenth century **PONTEFRACT** historian wrote several definitive studies of the town including *Pontefract: It's Name, Lords and Castle, The Sieges of Pontefract Castle* and *The Black Friars of Pontefract*.

HONORARY FREEMEN OF WAKEFIELD
Since 1880, twenty-four people, four army units and the Cathedral Chapter have been awarded the distinguished Freedom of Wakefield City. The distinguished list includes the names of Prime Minister Lloyd George, the industrialist and philanthropist Dale Carnegie, the supermarket pioneer and benefactor Samuel Canning **CHILDS**, Field Marshall Montgomery and local politician Sir Jack **SMART**.

HOOD, ROBIN
Legendary thirteenth century patriot, freedom fighter and outlaw who according to some chroniclers was born in Wakefield or one of its villages. His name is associated with a local rival named **GEORGE-A-GREEN** who was the pinder of Wakefield. The name Hod or Hood appears in Wakefield Court Rolls for 1277. One place frequently associated with the outlaw is **WENTBRIDG**E, its deeply wooded valley on the line of the **GREAT NORTH ROAD**, proving ideal for ambush.

Robin Hood, Scarlet and Little John. Pontefract

HOPE, DAVID
The Wakefield 'born and bred' ninety-sixth Archbishop of York. He was formerly the Archbishop of London and Wakefield. His heraldic arms incorporate the fleur-de-lis of his home city. He resigned the see in 2005 to become the vicar of St Margaret's Church in Ilkley.

HORBURY
Attractive village to the west to Wakefield, its fine collection of eighteenth century buildings including the magnificent church of St Peter and St Leonard. It was built between 1791 and 1793 by the architect John **CARR** at his own expense. He is buried there. Another local celebrity was Sabine **BARING-GOULD**. The village has a **BRASS BAND**.

HOW, WILLIAM WALSHAM

Wakefield's first bishop enthroned in 1888 after the passing of the Bishopric of Wakefield Act in 1878. His effigy lies in a chapel dedicated to his name in **WAKEFIELD CATHEDRAL**. He was a prodigious composer of hymns, his affinity and rapport with young people earning him the name the 'Children's Bishop.' His published works include *The Closed Door* – instructions and meditations given at various retreats and quiet days.

HOWARD, CATHERINE

During a royal visit to **PONTEFRACT CASTLE**, King Henry VIII's wife illicitly enjoyed the affections of her lover Thomas Culpepper. History suggests that their relationship had been adulterously consummated in the rose garden of the house of the Abbot of St Mary's in York. Their liaisons were discovered and they were both arrested at the castle, the hapless queen going to the block.

HOWARD, LUKE

Manufacturing chemist and pharmacist known as 'The Godfather of Clouds' in acknowledgment of his pioneering research into meteorology. Born in 1772, he was interested in the weather from an early age and although he never formally became a scientist, his inquisitive nature and abiding enthusiasm and passion for the subject prompted a series of illuminating lectures and papers, published works such as *On the Modification of Clouds, The Climate of London* and *Seven Lectures on Meteorology* (acknowledged as the first weather text book) leading to his election to the fellowship of the Royal Society in 1821. Inspired by the work of Linneaus, he devised a nomenclature for the identification of clouds...'cumulus...Latin for 'heap'...convex or conical heaps, increasing upward from a horizontal base – wool bag clouds; stratus...Latin for 'layer' ...a widely extended horizontal sheet, increasing from below; cirrus...Latin for 'curl of hair'...parallel, flexuous fibres extensible by increase in any or all directions; nimbus...Latin for 'rain'...a rain cloud...a cloud or systems of clouds from which rain is falling.' In 1842, he published an influential study entitled: *A cycle of eighteen years in the seasons of Great Britain; deduced from meteorological observations made at Ackworth in the West Riding of Yorkshire from 1824 to 1841; compared with others before made for a like period (ending with 1823) in the vicinity of London.* His popularisation of the weather inspired the canvases of Turner and Constable. Howard's second wife was from Pontefract and upon retirement from business, he bought an estate in **ACKWORTH** – Ackworth Court. A member of the Plymouth Brethren, he was driven by the ideals of Quakerism and similarly imbued,

a. *Cirrus.* b. *Cumulus.*   c. *Stratus.*   d. *Cirro Cumulus.*   e. *Cirro Stratus.*   f. *Cumulo Stratus.*   g. *Nimbus.*

Cloud nomenclature images from 1870. LMA

his daughter Rachel founded Ackworth's Howard School in 1833. Luke Howard died in 1864. Howard Drive, Cirrus View and Stratus Close in Ackworth are named after him.

HOWITT, WILLIAM

Popular and prolific writer of topographical guides, poems, novels and especially adventure books for boys. Howitt was educated at **ACKWORTH SCHOOL** between 1802 and 1806. His considerable output includes *The Boys Country Book, The Rural Life of England, Visits to Remarkable Places* and *History of Discovery in Australia*.

HULME JACK

Miner and self-taught photographer who compiled a rare social archive, capturing images of the mining communities around Fryston where he lived all his life. He became 'Mr Fryston' and, perhaps uniquely in the history of photography, spent over 50 years documenting just one square mile of his native village. His family came from Staffordshire, his mother bringing her 'secret' of making oatcakes to Yorkshire. 'Every Sunday morning she'd get up

Inside the Home and Colonial Store in Carlton Street, Castleford, 1950s.
Wakefield Cultural Services, Jack Hulme Collection. Courtesy of www.twixtaireandcalder.org.uk: The online archive of Wakefield District Images.

Men and children playing in the streets, Fryston, 1940s.
Wakefield Cultural Services, Jack Hulme Collection. Courtesy of www.twixtaireandcalder.org.uk: The online archive of Wakefield District Images.

at three o'clock, light the fire and start pouring the mixture onto a griddle...by the time the first lot of baking was ready, there would be a queue forming outside of the house.' Hulme's introduction to photography came when he was about fourteen years old. '...I was walking through **CASTLEFORD** market when I saw this little camera.' His skill and passion produced a unique archive of 20,000 photographs. To widespread acclaim, the **YORKSHIRE ART CIRCUS** first exhibited a selection of these publicly just before the photographers death in 1998, further exhibitions being held in the Royal Festival Hall in London, **FRYSTON** and elsewhere. The compilations, *World Famous Round Here – The Photographs of Jack Hulme* and *Jack Hulme - A Photographic Memory* are published by Yorkshire Art Circus. Each photograph is a social documentary with titles like *Mother Resting After Making Oatcakes*, *The Shift*, *Donkey Stoning the Step*, *Getting Washed at Home* and my particular favourite, *Jammy Face* showing a filthy but cherubic little tot covered in marmalade.

HUNTLEY, IAN

Convicted murderer of the schoolgirls Holly Wells and Jessica Chapman. The 'most hated man in Britain' was transferred to **WAKEFIELD PRISON** in 2004 and inducted to its special sex offender's treatment programme. Having previously attempted to take his own life, he was subjected to a suicide watch. Huntley's sentencing was deferred until September 2005 when a Judge imposed two life terms. He stipulated that although the killings did not meet the criteria for a 'whole life term' he recommended a 40-year term, suggesting that this offered 'little or no hope of release'.

I

INDUSTRIAL ESTATES/BUSINESS PARKS

Over forty serviced sites are operating throughout the district many with direct access to the A1 and the M1 and M62 Motorways. A plethora of information is available detailing grant and financial assistance regimes, site data, logistics and training options. All initial enquiries should be made through **WAKEFIELD FIRST**.

J

JACKSON, BRUCE

Fondly remembered Finance Officer with Wakefield MDC's Planning Department during the 1970s and 1980s, who advocated, in a descending order of enjoyment, the supreme attributes of sport, television and sex. He was very popular with colleagues for his use of 'Jacksonese', just three examples serving to illustrate his penchant for malapropism: 'I finished off my meal with a pudding: I had apple struggle.' 'I'm rather partial to Black Forest Ghetto.' 'The Lightweight Walk is a real test of endurance.'

JEPSON, CARL 'SPIKE'

The 2004 commanding officer and team leader of the RAF's elite aerobatic team The Red Arrows, 'Red One' was educated at **SILCOATES SCHOOL**, Wakefield where he was awarded an RAF Sixth Form Scholarship and an RAF Flying Scholarship. He learnt to fly long before he could drive.

JESUS CHAPEL, ACKWORTH GRANGE

Designed inside and out by Pugin, the most celebrated architect of his day, this 'Gem of the North' replicated chapels of the Edward III period with its fine tracery, decorated style, gilded extravagance and exuberant stained glass.

It was built in 1842 for the private use of the Tempest family and the small community of Ackworth Roman Catholics but demolished in 1966 in another senseless act of philistinism. Some of its treasures were preserved. Its reredos went to Campsall Church. Two sculptures were donated to a church in Doncaster and some glass found its way to Durham Cathedral.

K

KELLINGLEY COLLIERY
Miners sinking No. 2 Shaft plunged to a record depth of 336 feet in 31 days in January 1961.

KETTLETHORPE HALL
A two-storied, five-bay extravagance dating from 1727. Its lakeside boat-house and summer-house incorporates the worn façade from the **CHANTRY BRIDGE CHAPEL, WAKEFIELD**.

Kettlethorpe Hall. LMA

KIDCOTE PRISON
Dating from as early as 1278, kidcotes (referred to colloquially as kitty's) were local prisons set up in the larger towns during the Middle Ages. Wakefield had a kidcote in the Bull Ring. It was in the care of a constable who also had charge of the ducking stool, the stocks, the pillory and the gibbet. Prisoners were held in the kidcote pending punishment.

KING'S ARMS, HEATH
Seventeenth century heritage inn preserving a genuine Yorkshire range, flagstones, wainscoting and gaslights in the conservation village of Heath. The ghost of Lady **BOLLES** is reputed to haunt the bars.

KING'S OWN YORKSHIRE LIGHT INFANTRY

Famous Yorkshire regiment (incorporating the 51st and 105th Regiments of Foot) with battle honours throughout the world. It had barracks in **PONTEFRACT**. Divisions of the regiment have been granted the Freedom of Wakefield three times - in 1901, 1902 and 1945. The regimental museum is in Doncaster. The museum has an extensive display of medals and a model of the Pontefract barracks.

KINSLEY

A former mining village near **HEMSWORTH** predominantly made up of colliery owned terraced housing. The village became the national centre of attention during the Hemsworth Colliery miners strike in 1905. The mining company sought eviction orders from the court and many families – men, women and children – were forcibly removed from their homes by squads of policemen, although the mood was amazingly stoical and the opposition non-violent. The landlord of the Kinsley Hotel, Thomas Elstone, who took pity on the miners children and provided temporary accommodation in his ballroom, is shown in a famous postcard supervising a soup kitchen in the hotel yard. Other children were sent for temporary fostering in outlying villages but some joined their hard-pressed parents in church halls and in a tented encampment nearby. The *Barnsley Chronicle* reported: 'The prospect of a long period under canvas for the women and children is, however, a dark one at best particularly when one considers the approaching cold weather.' The evictions continued, the bobbies, blue eviction orders in hand, approaching the house of a musical man called Robert Battye – 'Concertina Bob' in Gorton Terrace. He had lived there eighteen years. Accompanied by his son on harp, Bob began playing *See The Conquering Hero Comes* followed immediately by *The Dead March*. The *Yorkshire Post* takes up the story: '...on the threshold stood the aged grandmother, her grey hairs turning white, with tears welling in her eyes at the thought of her home being broken up. Calm and collected to be the observer, the minstrel-miner was yet wracked with conflicting emotions. He kept on playing while the dozen or so policemen entered his home, tore down the pictures, removed the tables and chairs and pots and pans and dumped them all outside. And then, the kitchen cleared, Bob and his son appeared outside with the concertina and the harp and commenced again, while the police rummaged the bedrooms. Rubbing his wet eyes with his horny hand, the musician played *Home Sweet Home*. It was too much for him; he had to change the tune to keep his spirits up. And so in turn one heard snatches of *Bill Bailey*, *Hiawatha*, *The Lost Chord* and *Jolly Good Company*. Weak piping voices took up the choruses. There were voices of the women around full of tears. Meanwhile infants-in-arms whimpered, uncomfortable in the rain. 'Hush, there's a bobby man coming', one wife was

Police evicting miners and their families at Kinsley, October 1905.
Brian Elliott Collection

Wales. Photor.
Hemsworth

Oct. 3/05

heard to whisper to quieten her child, as she indicated a stout policeman who was engaged in dragging a big table out into the street. And so between laughter and tears, the ejectment went on, to the music of the miner-tenant and his son. Pennies were showered on them both as the police left them amid their furniture.' Such press pathos aroused enormous public outrage and sympathy and donations of money, provisions and clothing began steadily arriving in Kinsley. Politicians were also concerned at the plight of the families, the famous MP Keir Hardie visiting Kinsley and denouncing the evictions and urging everyone to vote Labour at the next General Election. In total, the dispute lasted a gruelling 188 weeks. But the agonies were not in vain. Wages and working conditions improved and subsequent legislation made it more difficult for colliery owners to evict tenants. And, locally, in Kinsley, miners got new housing.

KINSLEY GREYHOUND STADIUM
Popular, thrice-weekly 'grand nights out at the dogs'.

Kinsley Greyhound Stadium, 1967. Brian Elliott Collection

KIRKHAMGATE
A Wakefield satellite village, formerly consisting of farmsteads and pit cottages at the edge of the forested area known as the **OUTWOOD**. Gourmet forced **RHUBARB** is grown locally for despatch to Covent Garden and other specialist retailers in the spring.

KIRKTHORPE

Despite its proximity to the city of Wakefield, this village has a rural atmosphere, its ancient stocks, Frieston's Hospital Almshouses founded in 1595 and its St Peter's Church, setting a relaxed scene. In the churchyard is an unusual cluster of gravestones belonging to **FRENCH NUNS**.

KNOTTINGLEY

Industrial and transhipment centre on the **AIRE RIVER** traditionally producing glass containers and chemicals. Breweries, shipbuilding yards and limekilns were all once important to the local economy, vast numbers of barges tying up at wharves that gave the town the appearance of a sea port. At the close of the nineteenth century, the local skyline was sprouted with chimneys, one visitor describing the noisome watercourse full of the poison from 'vats and sewers and dye-houses' as the 'Yorkshire River Styx'. The olfactory courage needed to navigate this stream from Knottingley to Leeds is truly noble.' Today, the condition of the river is vastly improved, shoals of roach gracing the flow at Leeds Bridge and elsewhere. The town was the boyhood home of fearsome gunslinger Ben **THOMPSON**. A group of Bronze Age barrows survive in the vicinity of a town which has only limited architectural merit, only the church of St Botolph, an L - shaped period dwelling known as the White House and a residence in Jackson Lane described by Pevsner as 'a truly crazy performance' being worthy of note.

KNOTTINGLEY AND GOOLE CANAL

The 18½ miles waterway was opened in 1826. Built through practically level countryside, the canal needed few locks and could be used by the largest vessels for the shipment of coal, grain and timber.

KNOTTINGLEY KING'S MILLS

Water powered mills were the mainstays of the local economy since the eleventh century, several **KNOTTINGLEY** mills producing the monarch's corn after the **WARS OF THE ROSES**. Following the commercialisation of the waterways, conflicts arose between **BOATMEN** and millers, the diversions of flows to turn mill wheels causing river craft to run aground for lack of water. Bitter disputes went on for decades until the cutting of the **KNOTTINGLEY AND GOOLE CANAL** relieved the problem. Owned by the canal operating company, the King's Mills became the principal producer of flour in the area. **CORN** was, however, a commodity badly affected by the legislative consequences of the Napoleonic Wars and the mills fell into disrepair by the late 1830s, the company having to prevent a local quarryman from breaking up the access road to get to the limestone underneath! But the persistence of MP Richard **COBDEN** bore fruit and with changing fortunes, tenant William Jackson arrested the decline and enlarged and modernised the mills, the premises passing into the tenancy of John Croysdale. Although a major fire swept through the mill on 10th April 1884 – misted particles of flour are highly explosive - it survived to be further updated. It survives today as a conglomerate company. A pair of old millstones was donated to Knottingley Civic Society and erected at the eastern and western boundaries of the old urban district.

KNOTTINGLEY'S 'WISE MAN'

Unchallenged as a modern day Solomon, this eccentric sage was one day accosted by an opulent farmer who had been robbed of a cow. Anxious to know where his beast had gone, the farmer had previously enquired about the district, receiving the same and solemn suggestion: 'Go see yon Wise Man.' A humorous cove who always looked on the bright side of life, he feigned to accept the advice and presented himself at the wizard's temple in **KNOTTINGLEY** early one autumn morning. The oracle was in bed, so taking a length of timber and a bucket of water, the practical joker prepared a rude awakening, propping the log against the door with the bucket precariously perched on top. He then tapped away prising the sleeper from his bed. 'Who's there?' shouted the Wise Man. 'Be quick,' responded the farmer, 'and open the door. I want to see thee.' Half dressed, the prophet opened the door...and sploosh! The water went all over his head. 'Oh dear, oh dear! Who's done that?' he moaned getting to his feet. 'Na, na!' roared the farmer, bursting with laughter and jigging with delight at the wizard's plight and ignorance. 'If thoo can't tell me who did that, thoo can't tell me who stole my coo. Good morning!'

KNURR AND SPELL

An old English game known locally as 'Miners' Golf', this popular **WEST RIDING** game was much played in colliery villages. The South Yorkshire version – played around Barnsley – is know as Nipsy. The equipment consists of a small pot ball – the knurr – suspended above the ground in an open sling or on a springboard -and a flat ended bat – the spell. The object is to hit the airborne knurr with the spell and propel it as far as possible, upright sticks or stones spaced at 20 yards intervals serving to regulate the score. The game was usually attended by much betting. The game is illustrated in George Walker's book *The Costume of Yorkshire* published in 1814. In the 1960s and 1970s, Yorkshire Television organised World Championships.

Knurr and Spell, c.1895. Brian Elliott Collection

L

LAKE LOCK RAIL ROAD

Built around 1800 with a gauge of 3 feet 4 inches, it ran from **OUTWOOD** where numerous collieries existed to the river transhipment centre at **BOTTOMBOAT**. It is regarded as the first public railway. As well as coal, it carried road stone. In 1824, a 4 feet 5 inches gauge parallel track was added. Both lines were abandoned in the 1840s.

LAVATORIAL HUMOUR

'When I was at school in **HEMSWORTH**, the loos were dark and smelly and the walls were crumbling. They had pull cisterns and if I went in there when other people were in the building, I stood a strong chance of someone in the next cubicle standing on their loo and flushing mine from above – instants bidets!'

(P Guest)

'Although we had an inside lavatory upstairs in our house in **SOUTH ELMSALL**, I much preferred to go outside. One pitch-black night, I dashed out without thinking, eventually realising I'd not checked for paper. I fumbled and felt something shiny and slippery which I took to be a magazine and wiped away. Next day, my son—in—law who was a plumber, told me he'd lost one of his putty wrappers.'

(N Bell)

'I was frightened rigid. It had so many moving parts. After the old fashioned privy in our **OSSETT** yard, it was noisy and quite sinister.'
(B Levington remembering the installation of a device called the Duckett – an 'automatic slop water closet').

LEATHAM, WILLIAM

A Wakefield member of the **QUAKERS** and an eminent banker widely regarded for his expertise on fiscal policies and currency. In 1840 he published *Letters on the Currency*, which was influential in developing governmental strategies.

LEE FAIR

Ancient fair held at West **ARDSLEY** in August and September. One of the most important in England granted to the canons of **NOSTELL PRIORY**, the fair was celebrated for its size and importance, hundreds of cattle and horses and vast stocks of fruit and vegetables going on sale. The Wakefield Court Rolls reveal the presence of buyers from as far away as Newcastle, one entry recording the fun had by one William the Carter who overturned a stall, upsetting twenty gallons of beer worth 2 shillings and 4 pence and a cask valued at 12 pence.

LEE, JOHN
This prominent lawyer and entrepreneur born in 1759 initiated the **LAKE LOCK RAIL ROAD**. He developed the fashionable out-of-town **WAKEFIELD ST JOHN'S SQUARE** and lived there until his death in 1802.

LEGS ONCE A WEEK, BACKS ONCE A WEEK
Old miners' maxim referring to the common practice, before the advent of pithead baths, of only washing legs and backs once every seven days. After his shift, the homecomer would routinely wash his hands and forearms before sitting down to his meal. Before bedtime, his face and chest would receive attention ...but that would be it...unless it was a Lowbow day!

LEIDART
The innovative town of **PONTEFRACT** produced its own **ENGLAND'S** brand bicycle and, in the 1930s, a unique motor car with the Leidart marque. It was built in the Cornmarket garage of Leith Huddart and Co to the order of customer Pip Barran, the manager of the Snydale Brickworks. The vehicle was developed around a Ford V8 engine and a Bugatti chassis. Only one car was made with the registration number AWY 817.

LEIGHTON, KENNETH
A talented chorister, pianist and composer who was born in Wakefield in 1929. Leighton studied at the **WAKEFIELD QUEEN ELIZABETH'S GRAMMAR SCHOOL** and at Oxford and in Rome. He was one of the most celebrated post war composers producing over a hundred published works. A prolific prize winner, he was made an honorary fellow of the Royal College of Music in 1982. Just two months before his death in 1988, he acknowledged his debt to **WAKEFIELD CATHEDRAL** by attending a concert there to celebrate the centenary of the diocese.

LINDLEY, WILLIAM
He trained as an architect in the office of John **CARR** from the early 1750s until 1774. A Neo-classicist who developed his own practice, he designed houses in **WAKEFIELD SOUTH PARADE** and drew up plans for **ACKWORTH SCHOOL** Meeting House.

LINNECAR, RICHARD
Born in 1712, a versatile coroner, draper, wine merchant, postmaster, masonic lodge master, poet and dramatist, Linnecar settled in Wakefield in

1750, eventually moving to a large house in Little Westgate. In 1789 he published two comedy dramas – *The Lucky Escape* and *Plotting Wives*, a tragedy entitled *The Generous Moor* and various sonnets, songs and commentaries on freemasonry. His plays were performed at the local theatre in the early 1770s. He died as theatrically as he had lived whilst officiating at an inquest in 1800.

LIQUORICE

Exotic Mediterranean root plant first grown by **CLUNIAC MONKS** in the sandy soils of the Pontefract district. Cultivation reached its peak in the late 18th and early 19th centuries, the last crop dying in a Bondgate field in 1972 although specimen plants still survive in the area. The root was used to make Pontefract Cakes and the famous Liquorice Allsorts both of which can still be bought locally. At one time, there were four sweet factories in the town, the constant perfume of boiling confectionery drifting down every street. Hundreds of local factory girls would wear their distinctive turbans. The delicacy also coats a locally produced cheese and is used to flavour beer. The delicacy has celebrity connections. In Chaplin's film *Goldrush*, he eats his own liquorice bootlaces. The character 'Jaws' in the James Bond epic *Moonraker* bites through a cable car cable made from braided liquorice. And Spencer Tracy in *Adam's Rib* frightens Katherine Hepburn by pretending to shoot himself in the mouth with a chewy gun. He bites off the barrel and says: 'I just can't resist liquorice!'

Liquorice bush. Pontefract Museum   *Workman in a liquorice field.* Pontefract Museum

Pontefract Cake stamper. Pontefract Museum

LIVINGSTONE, DOCTOR DAVID

This eminent medical missionary and African explorer who discovered the source of the Zambezi river, came to Yorkshire in 1859 and gave a lecture on his adventures at **ACKWORTH SCHOOL**. Soon afterwards, he returned to the Dark Continent where he died in 1873.

LIZARDS

Apart from exotic examples of the species displayed in Squire Waterton's collection in **WAKEFIELD MUSEUM** and certain human reptilian forms that stalk the lounges of particular city clubs and bars, lizards are uncommon in the district. But remarkably, according to folk tale, one live representative of the genus was discovered locally in a lump of coal in 1818. The animal was found by a miner in a solid block of coal 150 feet below ground in the colliery of William Fenton at **OUTWOOD**. When exposed to the air, the creature promptly died.

LOFTHOUSE GATE

Its railway bridge is unique in carrying two railway routes and a public highway over another railway built below.

LOFTHOUSE, GEOFFREY, LORD

Local Labour MP and, uniquely at different times, the Deputy Speaker of both the House of Commons and the House of Lords. A former **FEATHERSTONE** miner who began work at the coalface at the age of fourteen and spent fourteen years in the industry, he went on to become a prominent trade unionist, his zeal, ambition, commitment to obtaining degree qualifications and passion for his constituents propelling him into politics. His book *Coal Sack to Woolsack* was published in 1999, *A Very Miner MP* following soon after. A big influence in his life was his grandfather whose sound advice he followed all his life: 'Always trust your own. If they can't do anything for thee...there's not much bloody chance the others will.'

LOFTHOUSE PARK

Sixty acres amusement and pleasure park at **LOFTHOUSE GATE** opened to fanfares in June 1908 by the directors of the Wakefield and District Light Railway Company. The *Wakefield Herald* trumpeted the attraction in an article '...and already the place has been metamorphosed from a gentleman's park to a White City of imposing dimensions'. The park was packed with every conceivable modern attraction and was linked with Wakefield and Leeds by tramways, cars arriving at the park gates every two minutes! It offered a 40 feet high wooden helter-skelter, two aerial rides, a house of mirrors, a fun house, a maze and a 1000-seat pavilion housing shops, a dance floor and cinema screens. Adjacent was a glass-and-iron-framed winter garden planted with palm trees and exotic plants and a roller skating rink. Other sensational features included an African village peopled by 'real' Abyssinians in native huts and a spectacular crash stunt involving an open touring car and a ramp, several men careering down the slope and screaming

Lofthouse Park Pavilion. The John Goodchild Collection. Courtesy of www.twixtaireandcalder.org.uk: The online archive of Wakefield District Images

in fear as their vehicle hit the buffers and somersaulted three times onto a mattress. Variety shows were held in the pavilion, there were 'sundry scientific marvels' and art exhibitions and the Blackburn Aeroplane Company built a large hanger offering monoplane flights. A zoo exhibiting lions, tigers and bears was later added to the park's attractions. At the beginning of the First World War, the park was commandeered by the government and used as an internment camp – the **ZIVILINTERNIERUNGLASGER**. After the war the park became derelict and the pavilion was eventually destroyed by fire.

LOFTHOUSE PIT DISASTER

On 21st March 1973, Face South 9B in the Flockton Thin Seam was flooded by a deadly inrush of water from old workings. Despite desperate rescue attempts involving the use of pumps and frogmen, seven men died and only one body was ever recovered. At the time of the disaster, 837 underground workers and 207 surface workers were producing 18,500 tons of coal per week. In May 1973, an eight-day public inquiry was held in Wakefield. Among the witness was Arthur **SCARGILL**, the President of the National Union of Mineworkers.

'LORD HAW HAW':

Wartime traitor whose real name was William Joyce. He once, allegedly, lived at **ROGERTHORPE MANOR** near **BADSWORTH**. An American citizen and a naturalised German, Joyce became a senior member of the British Union of Fascists. Fearing internment at the outbreak of World War Two, acting on a tip-off, he fled to Germany and worked as a propagandist broadcaster on Radio Berlin. He succeed Wolf Mitler whose verbal delivery and accent had been described by the *Daily Express* as '…of the haw-haw, dammit-get-out-of-my-way variety.' The reference stuck, and from September 1939 until April 1945, 'Lord Haw Haw's' catchphrase 'Germany calling …Germany calling' was heard all over Britain on medium wave radio and in the United States on the short wave. Ironically, Joyce's broadcasts proved his undoing. He was captured in disguise by British troops who immediately recognised his voice. Ordinarily, his American and German connections would have thwarted a conviction for treason. But having lied about his nationality to obtain a British passport, he was found guilty on a technicality and executed in January 1946 by Yorkshireman Albert Pierrepoint who, three years later hanged John George **HAIGH**. Pierrepoint had previously executed Edwin Sowerby, the murderer of Jane **DARWELL**.

LUND, JOHN

A largely uneducated Pontefract barber who in 1776 took up the quill between shaves to produce a humorous and locally popular literary work entitled *The Newcastle Rider* or *Ducks and Green Pease*. Another notable production was *A Collection of Oddities in Prose and Verse by a very Odd Author*.

M

MACDONALD, JANE

Wakefield singer first 'discovered' in 1998 on a 'reality TV' documentary *The Cruise* about the life of working people on a cruise ship. New-found fame propelled the singer to mini-stardom, her retro-style becoming popular on television and in live theatre shows throughout the country.

MALKIN, HARRY

Former mechanical fitter who worked in **FRYSTON COLLIERY** for twenty years but left after the strike of 1984/85. A talented artist, he won a prize in a national art competition in 1986, becoming a professional in 1989. Specialising in the noir depiction of life underground, he is the artist in residence at the **YORKSHIRE ART CIRCUS**.

MANGNALL, RICHMAL

This remarkable woman was born in Manchester in 1769. Always short in stature – she never grew above four feet in height – she was sent to school at Crofton Hall. She was a diligent pupil who finally became the academy's mistress, being described by contemporaries as 'a most excellent and honourable lady'. Mangnall wrote poetry in her spare time and produced a popular and extraordinarily successful guide that was widely used in schools throughout the land. The advice in *Historical Questions for the Use of Young People* - generally known as Mangnall's Questions - 'to lead them to a habit of reflection and observation for themselves', was widely influential. Mangnall's philosophies, which were far in advance of her time, have a profound resonance with educational academia to this day. Her portrait by John Downman is in the National Portrait Gallery in London.

MARRIOTT, WILLIAM THOMAS

The third generation of a family of colliery owners and worsted spinners, with premises at Westgate End in Wakefield, Marriott was an able and generous man who was well respected by his workers. When he died in 1899, he left a fortune of £212,000 and a fine collection of antiquities and art works at his Sandal Grange home. At the time of his death, his business was described as 'one of the most prosperous manufacturing enterprises in England.'

At one time, Wakefield was a major clothing centre. LMA

MARSDEN, JOHN
This prominent Wakefield lawyer, estate manager and colliery owner opened Woolley Colliery in 1853. In the 1850s he also undertook a modernisation of the Denby Grange Colliery, installing its innovative railway, which linked the pit to Calder Grove. He secured the office of Solicitor to the West Riding and lived in some style at Walton House on the outskirts of the town.

MARSLAND, JOSEPH
Worsted spinner and colliery proprietor who developed the New Victoria Colliery and the Providence Colliery in Balne Lane, Wakefield in the 1850s. He endowed Marsland's Almshouses on Primrose Hill for 'poor deserving females.'

MEE, MICHAEL CLIVE
Local hero who gave his life to rescue a young girl on 28 December 1995. On that cold Thursday morning, Tracy Pattison and her friend Jemma were exercising a friend's dogs on the banks of **HEMSWORTH WATER PARK** lake, one animal scampering out onto the frozen ice. The ice broke and the dog got into difficulties, Jemma setting off to get help as Tracy attempted to assist the dog. She too fell into the water. Off-duty Barnsley fire-fighter Michael Mee was walking in the park with his wife and daughter and he heard the cries for help. He despatched his daughter to telephone the fire brigade, removed some clothing and crawled out on the ice in an attempt to reach the girl who was about 100 feet from the bank. His weight fractured the surface and he too fell into the water, which was about seven feet deep. By this time, several concerned people had congregated on the bank and two more men joined the rescue attempt. One man, like Tracy and Michael before him, plunged into the water, the third man attempting to wade out and break the ice as he got nearer the stricken three. The extreme cold and the unexpected depth drove the man back and he stood shivering on the bank as all three people disappeared under the surface and drowned. Three bodies were later recovered. In recognition of Mee's heroic act, his name was honoured with enrolment in the Roll of Honour of the Carnegie Hero Fund Trust.

'MEET ME IN RED'
Popular phrase of assignation, visitors to Wakefield rendezvousing in the Red Café Bar and Restaurant in the George and Crown Yard off Upper Westgate.

MENAGERIES
In the middle of the nineteenth century menageries and circuses toured the major county towns, satisfying the public fascination for wild and exotic animals. On 3 and 4 November 1894, Mander's Grand National Star Menagerie entered

CASTLEFORD and **PONTEFRACT** in a brilliant procession headed by Martini Maccomo, the great African lion tamer. In the cavalcade were lions, tigers, panthers, leopards, gorillas, polar bears, camels, hyenas, 'half a thousand other animals from all parts of the known world' and, it was claimed, a unicorn 'never seen in this country before, and positively the only one in Europe.' For an admission of one shilling (children under ten sixpence), spectators could marvel at an elephant playing the piano, Punch and Judy riding on elephants and jumping hurdles and an elephant playing the trombone.

MERCER, DAVID, STUART

Born the son of a railwayman in Portobello, Wakefield in 1928, Mercer failed his eleven-plus examination and left school at the age of fourteen to work as a laboratory assistant. He joined the Merchant Navy, enrolled as a student in Wakefield and Durham and began writing short stories, achieving modest success in 1960. His perseverance paid off in 1961 when his play, *Where the Difference Ends* was accepted by BBC Television. A subsequent play, *A Suitable Case for Treatment* was adapted for a film staring Vanessa Redgrave. During the next decade he played a prominent role in bringing realistic drama to the small screen but he was perennially frustrated that his visceral style was unsuitable for the theatre and was disappointed that his work never became a catalyst for social justice. He died in Israel in 1980.

MERRIE CITY

Wakefield is noted for its merriment, the reputation dating from the time of Edward IV who became the first king of the **YORKISTS** after the Battle of Towton in 1461. Rejoicing at the success of their Lord of the Manor, the citizens indulged in games, sports and amusements of all kinds, including bull and bear baiting, archery, cock-fighting, bowls, dancing, drinking and springtime dalliances, the fun continuing to the present day in feats of rollicking endurance epitomised by the **WESTGATE RUN**.

METHLEY HALL

Much altered mansion with attendant ranges near **CASTLEFORD** with many architectural gems including oriel windows, rainwater heads and carved wooden screens. Dating from the fifteenth century with substantial additions during the sixteenth, seventeen and nineteenth centuries, the estate was bought by Sir John Savile in 1588. A suite of rooms along the southeast front of the building was rebuilt by John **CARR** before 1778. Sadly the hall was demolished in 1963 but an imposing tomb chest dedicated to Sir John Savile and his son Sir Henry Savile survives in the nearby St Oswald's Church. The church has other treasures, notably a circa 1500 lectern and several alabaster **EFFIGIES**.

MICKMAN, PHILIP

This tireless and talented merman from **OSSETT**, the son of a director of the town's Mickman's Hosiery Company, was born in 1931. He was only a modest pupil at the **WAKEFIELD QUEEN ELIZABETH'S GRAMMAR SCHOOL** but he excelled as a swimmer, spending long hours training in Wakefield's Sun Lane pool. With ambitions to swim the English Channel, in the winter of 1948/49, he practised in Ossett's Healey Mill Dam to acclimatise to the expected low sea temperatures. Undaunted after four abortive attempts at a crossing, he began swimming from Cap Griz Nez on the French coast on 23 August 1949. After sixteen hours, despite strong tides, he managed to get within a few miles of Folkestone but currents took him fourteen miles away from his goal toward Deal. Ignoring the advice of his father to quit, the indefatigable Mackman continued swimming and made landfall near Deal after being in the water for an incredible 23 hours and 48 minutes – the longest time ever recorded for a cross-channel swim. He had swum an estimated forty miles! A week later, he was honoured with a civic reception in his home town and was presented with a message of congratulation from the king, an illuminated address and a waterproof watch! On 1 September 1952, he was back in the water again, setting out from England. Adverse conditions persuaded the man in the pilot boat to abandon the attempt but his charge struck out for Calais where the mayor greeted him after 18 hours 44 minutes. At just twenty-one years of age, Mickman became the youngest person to swim the Channel in both directions. Ironically, the swimmer went to Cambridge to read science in 1952 and he graduated in 1955. He spent much of his later life in Scarborough where he became a colourful local character and businessman. He died there in 1996.

Phil Mickman (right of mayor) being presented with a certificate, 1949.
Wakefield Cultural Services, Fowler Collection. Courtesy of www.twixtaireandcalder.org.uk: The online archive of Wakefield District Images

MILESTONE
The oldest milestone in the district was erected in AD 249 when Trainaus was Emperor of Rome. It was sited in **CASTLEFORD** at the junction of important military highways linking York and Chester. Lost for centuries, it was discovered in the grounds of a house in the early 1880s and was eventually acquired for display in Leeds. Aggrieved at the perceived theft, local people agitated for its return in the 1920s. After nearly thirty years of lobbying, the relic was returned in 1957. It had now has pride of place in **PONTEFRACT MUSEUM** pending a return home once facilities permit.

MILNES, JAMES
This prominent member of a local textile family, which included Pemberton **MILNES**, was born in 1755. In 1778, he married the daughter of a Leeds cloth merchant and gleefully accepted a dowry of £100,000 with more money promised on the death of his father-in-law. His fortune enabled him to commission a large brick mansion just outside Wakefield called **THORNES HOUSE**. A philanthropist and educational reformer with interests in literature and science, he became Deputy Lieutenant of the West Riding and, in 1802, just three years before his death, the MP for Bletchingley in Surrey.

MILNES, PEMBERTON
A prosperous eighteenth century textile merchant whose family business supplied cloth to the Russian armies. In the 1790s, he was one of only nine Wakefield gentlemen to own a four-horse carriage, his considerable income enabling him build a town house, Milnes House (Pemberton House) a still prominent edifice adjacent to the railway station approach. Milnes was a politically controversial figure who was on intimate terms with fellow dissenting Whig, the Second Marquess of Rockingham, who became Prime Minister in 1756. Milnes supported the cause of the secessionist American colonies and lauded the aims of the French Revolution, several outraged opponents threatening to burn his palatial home. A sumptuously appointed building, it was described as having: 'rich carving and plasterwork after the designs of Gibbons.' His detached garden, now known as the **ORANGERY**, passed over to his daughter when he died in 1795.

MILNES, RICHARD MONCKTON
This prominent poet and MP for **PONTEFRACT** lived at Fryston Hall. He became Lord Houghton and famously proposed marriage to Florence Nightingale. She rejected his advances and devoted her life to a career in nursing.

MINERS' MEMORIES

King Coal once dominated the economic and social life of the district, thousands of men and generations of families living in the shadow of the big wheel. Mining was arduous, poorly paid, dangerous and damaging to health but the industry was renowned for solidarity, camaraderie and spiky humour. Memory still hews a rich seam.

'There were men in their eighties down there. We used to take bets on when one bloke of eighty-three would collapse.'

'When some blokes were asked to do a bit o' shovelling they came over all faint. There was more work in an Asprin.'

'Deputies are like bananas. They start off green; then they go yellow and finally they go rotten.'

'When they first opened the pithead baths, the old colliers would never wash their backs. They thought it would make them weak, so they only washed at weekends.'

"At the end of the shift, they'd scrape the floor along the face and sweep it. The deputy would look along the 200 yard face and say, 'I only want to see one.' All the props had to be in line. If any were out, he'd put half-inch chalk marks on the floor and they had to be moved. "

'I've been dead for four years but I continue to walk around. It's too expensive to die.'

'When my granddad came home from work, he'd gargle and spit the black pit muck into the pot sink.'

" 'I was down the pit bottom with one of the charge hands who spoke really posh. So I said to him, 'I going over there to relieve myself.' He said, 'But you do that every morning.' 'Doesn't thou?' I replied. 'No,' he answered, 'I go every nine days. I said, 'Tha dirty bugger; no wonder tha breath smells.' "

'If you'd been on a hard seam and not earned owt, you had to queue to see the manager on a Friday to ask for some '**BUTTY MONEY**'.

'Colliers Monday. That's when you didn't work Mondays when it was a nice day.'

'The most difficult place to remove the coal muck from was around the eye-lashes.'

"Before they opened the pithead baths, there was this fellow who, after his shift, used to call at his fancy woman's on his way home. He always ended up with a clean bit. One day his wife asked how every part of his body was black except that bit. He replied, 'I called at the toilet on the way home and washed there.' To make sure he wouldn't get caught again, he used to get his dusty cap and blacken himself again before he got home."

Mining was always a precarious and perilous occupation and there were dozen of fatalities in the industry every week. Miners' children would recite a little prayer to keep their fathers' safe:

> *Don't go down the mine dad,*
> *Dreams very often come true;*
> *Daddy, you know it would break my heart,*
> *If anything happened to you.*

DON'T GO DOWN THE MINE, DAD (No. 2).
"Don't go down in the mine, Dad,
Dreams very often come true;
Daddy, you know it would break my heart,
If anything happened to you;
Just go and tell my dream to your mates,
And as true as the stars that shine,
Something is going to happen to-day,
Dear Daddy, don't go down the mine!"

Don't Go Down the Mine, Dad.
Brian Elliott Collection

MINSTHORPE COMMUNITY COLLEGE
This Specialist Science College at **SOUTH ELMSALL** trains over 1800 students, supplementary services embracing adult education and training, childcare and family learning and sports and fitness.

MIRACLE PLAYS
Developed from liturgical ritual, especially the annual pageant of Corpus Christi, the plays were a lay interpretation of scriptural stories and the lives of the saints (non-Biblical themes were later introduced) performed in the open air on a wheeled stage or on platforms erected along a processional route. In Wakefield, the very popular plays were held in the churchyard at the time of the annual fair, which was first granted by King John in 1204. Both Wakefield and York had prominent annual play cycles, Wakefield offering interpretations on subjects such as the Nativity, Noah and the Flood and the Resurrection. The plays were invested with much local colour and not a little levity, the Wakefield Second Shepherds' Play opening:

> *Lord, but this weather is cold, and I am ill wrapped,*
> *My hand's in frost's hold, so long have I napped;*
> *My legs they fold, my fingers are chapped,*
> *It is not as of old, for I am lapped*
> *In sorrow...*

Written between 1350 and 1450, some of the play manuscripts have survived and are kept in the Huntington Library of San Marino in California. Several plays were reproduced in Wakefield Park during the Festival of Britain in 1951. In 1961 a new edition of the plays was published and later performed at the Mermaid Theatre in London.

MONTGOMERY, BERNARD, FIELD MARSHALL

World War Two commander of British troops in North Africa and Europe. He visited Wakefield in 1947 to receive the Freedom of the City, his cavalcade receiving a rapturous reception by residents who draped buildings lining the route with bunting and national flags.

MOORE, HENRY

Internationally acclaimed sculptor born in Roundhill Road, **CASTLEFORD** in 1898. Inspired by an influential teacher, he decided to become a sculptor at the age of eight and went on to study at the Leeds School of Art – where he met Barbara **HEPWORTH** – and the Royal College of Art in London. His first commission was *West Wind* (1928) a relief set into the façade of London Underground's HQ at 55 Broadway, London. He specialised in abstract representations of the human female body deriving some of his inspirations from local rock formations in places like Adel Woods in Leeds and also from Mayan culture. He helped define modernism, suggesting that art 'should have a certain mystery and should make demands on the spectator.' **WAKEFIELD ART GALLERY** exhibits an earthy and

Reclining figure 1936 by Henry Moore. Extract from Wakefield MDC's official guide

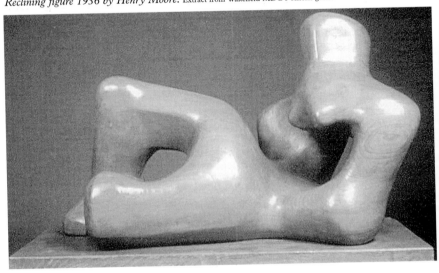

visceral collection of his etchings including the ethnically notable *Pit Boys at Pithead* (1942) and *Four Grey Sleepers* (1941). He is honoured in Leeds by a dedicated Henry Moore Gallery, in **CASTLEFORD** by a sculptural acclamation marking the site of his demolished home and by a reclining figure displayed outside the Civic Centre and extensively, in the grounds of the **YORKSHIRE SCULPTURE PARK**. Elsewhere, examples of his considerable output span the globe.

MORRIS, COLONEL JOHN

A Royalist stalwart during the English Civil War and the Governor of **PONTEFRACT CASTLE**, Morris hailed from **SOUTH ELMSALL** where he lived in Hague Hall. The Roundheads asserted 'that God had given him his abilities but the Devil the application of them.' He saw service in Ireland where he was twice wounded. After the king's capture he was involved in a ruse to retake the castle from the enemy. The dashing colonel arranged with a sympathetic sentry to turn a blind eye to eight discreetly placed scaling ladders. On the night of the assault, however, the unfortunate sentry was so drunk that the attempt was called off. But not before the alarm had been raised. The concerned castle governor immediately ordered all troops billeted in the town to return to sleep in the barracks. And he promised each man a new mattress. Morris saw his chance on 3 June 1648. With eight comrades who, were similarly disguised as tinkers, he sallied forth to the drawbridge peddling beds and provisions from a number of carts. The trick worked. With pistols hidden beneath their cloaks, Morris and his band were admitted. And then, as bold as brass, they gave the guards money and told them to go fetch some beer! Within no time, there were five hundred Royalists inside. Cromwell was not amused. He ordered General Rainsborough to besiege the stronghold, the general threatening to execute the captured Royalist hero Sir Marmaduke Langdale against the castle walls if there was any resistance. Inflamed, Morris rode out with twenty- two accomplices and galloped to Doncaster. His mission? To capture Rainsborough and make him a hostage! But the general was killed in a skirmish, the band returning to the castle to endure a long siege conducted, at first, by Cromwell himself. The besieger wrote the following terse letter to Morris on 9 November 1648:

For the Governor of Pontefract Castle

Sir- being come hither for the reduction of this place, I thought fit to summon you to deliver your Garrison to me, for the use of the Parliament. Those gentlemen and soldiers with you may have better terms than if you should hold it to extremity. I expect your answer this day and rest,
Your servant
OLIVER CROMWELL

Morris responded the same day:

Sir – I am confident you do not expect that I should pass my answer before I be satisfied that the summoner has power to perform my conditions, which must be confirmed by Parliament. Besides, the dispute betwixt yourself and Sir Henry Cholmley, commander in chief by commission of the committee of the militia of Yorkshire, who, as I am informed, denies all subordination to your authority. When my understanding is cleared in this concerning scruple, I shall endeavour to be as modest in my reply, as I have read you in your summons.

Sir, your servant,

JOHN MORRIS

Pontefract Castle, Nov, 9, 1648
For Lieutenant-General Cromwell

Following this rebuke, the shortage of food became pressing and forays were made into the countryside, one audacious snatch capturing 300 cattle from an enemy herd in **KNOTTINGLEY**. Eventually, hunger and a lack of ammunition and powder prevailed. After their capitulation in 1649, an amnesty was granted to all the defenders apart from six. But Morris and five of his friends were given a sporting chance and it was agreed that the gates would be opened. If they escaped a fusillade of fire and managed to ride five miles from the castle …they might live! The six men burst out from the castle and one was immediately brought down and killed. Three men retreated back inside and were rushed into the sally port where they were eventually walled up as the rest of the pardoned garrison left. Cromwell's troops searched high and low for the men but failed to find them. Eventually, they emerged to freedom. As for Morris and his friend Lieutenant Michael Blackburne - they escaped the melee at the drawbridge and made it as far as Lancaster, only to be betrayed and captured as they inquired in disguise about a ship. They were finally immured in York Castle, tried and sentenced to death. Tantalisingly, someone smuggled a rope into their cell and the pair began climbing down. Morris reached the ground comfortably and was urged by supporters to hurry to reach a tethered horse nearby. But the unfortunate Blackburne fell and broke his leg and was unable to continue. The twenty-nine-year-old Morris could have escaped but he stayed with his friend. Just before his execution, Morris uttered a final statement: 'I bless God I'm thought worthy to suffer for his name and for so good a cause; and if I had a thousand lives, I'd willingly lay them down for the cause of the king.' On 22 August, both men were brutally hanged, drawn and quartered. Portraits of the noble Morris are in the front of this book and in Sledmere Hall near Bridlington. He was buried at Wentworth.

MORTEN, MARGARET

Resident of Kirkthorpe accused in 1651 of witchcraft by a Joanne Booth of Warmfield. She claimed that her child became ill following Morten's offering of a piece of bread. She also alleged that her milk would not curdle when making butter or cheese. The evidence was deemed serious enough to mount an investigation, an incriminating examination of the suspect's thigh revealing two damning black spots. Morten was hauled before the Assizes but was acquitted.

MOTTYS

Numbered shift identification labels or metal tally discs used on coal tubs to identify which miner produced the load. Some were made of glued paper and had to be dampened with blackened tongues, but Motty Men would always be served first by sympathetic bar maids.

MOYNIHAN, ANDREW

This winner of the Victoria Cross was born in Wakefield. He joined the 90th Regiment – The Perthshire Volunteers and 'personally encountered and killed five Russians and rescued a wounded officer under heavy fire' during an assault on the Redan fortress at Sebastopol in 1854.

MULBERRY BUSH

A singular horticultural oddity in the yard of **WAKEFIELD PRISON**. Inmates would be made to run around the bush in daily exercise, the practice being set to verse in the childrens' ditty: 'Here we go round the mulberry bush, the mulberry bush, the mulberry bush; Here we go round the mulberry bush on a cold and frosty morning.'

N

NATIONAL COAL MINING MUSEUM FOR ENGLAND

Adapted from the former Caphouse Colliery at Overton, the museum graphically illustrates the lives of miners and their families. Attractions include pit ponies, an underground coalface tour and audio-visual plasma screen displays depicting miners at home, on the pit surface and at play.

NAVIGATION, THE

Popular former bargees public house of 1838 on the canal side at Calder Grove.

NAYLER (OR NAYLOR), JAMES

Born in1616 in East **ARDSLEY**, he served, during the Civil War, as a quartermaster in the Parliamentary Army. In 1651 he became a preacher for the **QUAKERS** and toured the country, according to one fantastical report, raising a woman from the dead in Exeter Gaol. His fame spread and he assumed the persona of the Messiah, his deluded followers strewing leaves and branches before him. He was eventually charged with blasphemy and whipped through the streets and pilloried and his tongue was pierced with a red-hot iron. A branded 'B' on his forehead proclaimed his sin to the entire world. Released from prison in 1659, he set out for Wakefield but died on his journey. His publications are *An Exhortation to the Rulers - the Preachers and Lawyers 1653, Milk for Babies and Meat for Strong Men, Nayler's Salutation to the Seed of God, 1656* and *An Answer to Blome's Fanatic History.*

NAYLOR, MARTIN, JOSEPH

This Cambridge university educated clergyman, lecturer, headmaster, political radical, freemason and editor from Batley Carr was renowned for calling a spade a 'bloody shovel', 'the only person in the university who was in the habit of using violent bad language when talking on political subjects.' Born in 1764, he became a curate in Wakefield, headmaster of its grammar school and editor of the *Wakefield Star,* his thirty years in charge, influencing liberal politics throughout the Calder valley and contributing to the passage of the Reform Act of 1832. A well-respected agitator and local reformer whose impulsiveness prevented him from climbing the ecclesiastical ladder, he died as the rector of **CROFTON** in 1843.

NEEDLE'S EYE
See **PYRAMIDAL LODGE**.

NELSON, BILLY

The son of a cab driver born in 1898 in Gill's Yard, Wakefield, Nelson started his working life as a miner at Low Laithes Colliery but at the age of fourteen he entered show business, appearing in a revue at the **WAKEFIELD HIPPODROME** called *The Four Hussar Girls and the Sentry.* At just 4′ 11″ high, he was something of an improbable lookout! After joining a circus in 1919 he formed a double-act with Duggie Wakefield and became part of a touring show *Boys will be Boys,* the boys in question, performing an act that became famous. In a sketch called *The New Garage,* the bumbling pair became hopelessly entangled in a mesh of car inner tubes and set out in a rickety old vehicle that fell apart. In 1933, Nelson appeared with his sidekick in Gracie Fields film *This Year of Grace.* He toured the USA, joined the cast in two notable films *Look Up and Laugh* and *Calling All Crooks* and, as the diminutive dame, starred in local revues and pantomimes, occasionally at the **WAKEFIELD**

OPERA HOUSE. Nelson died in 1977 but his son, Billy Morris, took the part of Just William in the 1940s BBC radio series of the same name.

NELSON'S COLUMN

A **PONTEFRACT** plaster cast in the Court Room of the old Town Hall in Gillygate, has a curious connection with the world famous monument in Trafalgar Square, London. The cast was used to mould one of the four panels displayed on the base of the monument. It shows the admiral mortally wounded on the deck of HMS *Victory*. Benjamin Oliveira MP was a friend of Carew, the sculptor of the panel. He offered the panel to the council in an ambiguously worded letter. The council enthusiastically agreed to the offer but members recoiled in horror when they received a bill! The expenditure rancoured with politicians, the warning 'Remember the Trafalgar memorial!' echoing round their debating chambers for years.

NETHERTON

Semi-rural village near the picturesque **COXLEY VALLEY**. Once noted for its sandstone quarries and for coal extraction, based originally on 'bell mining' from as early as 1401. Hope Pit was sunk in 1870 eventually becoming Denby Grange, which was linked with Caphouse Colliery (now the **NATIONAL COAL MINING MUSEUM FOR ENGLAND**) by a mineral railway. Hartley Bank Colliery was sunk in 1881 and closed in 1968. Netherton Hall is reputed to be haunted by a spectre in a grey dress, history recording its use by Oliver Cromwell during the Civil War.

NESTLE ROWNTREE

Conglomerate cereals and confectionery company based in **CASTLEFORD** where they produce one billion After Eight Mints every year.

NEVISON'S LEAP

A place on the Ferrybridge Road, **PONTEFRACT** – near the base of a twelfth century boundary cross – where the outlaw **NEVISON** boldly jumped across the road-cutting with one bound of his horse, to escape his pursuers.

NEVISON, WILLIAM (SOMETIMES JOHN), 'SWIFT NICK'

Highwayman in the mould of Robin **HOOD** born in **PONTEFRACT** in 1639. Given his nickname by Charles II, he made the legendary ride in one day in 1676 from London to York to establish an alibi. His feat was erroneously later attributed to Dick Turpin. A frequent visitor to **WENTBRIDGE** (the *Gate Inn* was one of his favourite 'stations') and Wakefield, the villain, with a price on his head, was arrested by Captain

William Hardcastle in the *Three Houses Inn* in **SANDAL MAGNA** in March 1684 and taken to a prison in York. He was found guilty of the crime of attempted murder and executed on the gallows the following May. He allegedly made a farewell speech to the judge who sentenced him, his words finding their way into a popular song:

> *All the years that I rode on the highway,*
> *I always had money in store,*
> *But whatever I took from the rich*
> *I freely gave back to the poor.*
> *But my peace I've made with my Maker,*
> *And my last ride I'm willing to go,*
> *So adieu to this world and its follies,*
> *For I'm ready to suffer the law.*

The author Daniel Defoe immortalised the highwayman as Mr Nicks in his book *A Tour Through the Whole Island of Great Britain*. At the time of his arrest in the inn, Nevison was asleep in a chair. That chair was donated by the arresting captain and is now preserved in St Helen's Church in Sandal Magna. The outlaw is buried in the grounds of St Mary's Church in Castlegate, York.

NEW HALL

Designed by the famous Robert Smythson, an impressive towered mansion near **PONTEFRACT CASTLE** built by the Seventh Earl of Shrewsbury in 1591 using stone from the nearby priory of the **CLUNIAC MONKS**. It played a prominent role in the Civil War sieges – it was abandoned by the Royalists on 19 November 1648 and left ablaze to deny shelter to the enemy. The Roundheads extinguished the fire and the building survived until its demolition in 1965. The old hall, which had thwarted the barrage of cannons, was assaulted using tractors and hawsers but it resisted to the end and had to be brought down with dynamite! In the district's woefully short-sighted rush to destruction – the demolition of **SIX CHIMNEYS** in Wakefield and the house of Henry **MOORE** in **CASTLEFORD** loom large – it lost a unique building that was described as one of the most magnificent Elizabethan mansions in England. At the time of its levelling, a preservation order was in force. Ironically, stone was removed for use in the foundations of the A1 viaduct in **WENTBRIDGE**.

NEWLAND HALL

Demolished around 1918, the hall near **NORMANTON** was built around 1745 to designs which were probably those of Robert Carr, the father of the more famous son. It was built on an estate at an important crossing point of the **CALDER RIVER** formerly occupied in the thirteenth century by a

The old corn mill at Newmillerdam. Brian Elliott Collection

preceptory of the Knights of St John. The area became dominated by mining operations begun when the first shafts were sunk in the 1860s, vast quantities of extracted coal, sand and gravel creating a void currently exploited as the **WELBECK LANDFILL** scheme.

NEWMILLERDAM

Taking its name from a corn mill established in the area round 1285 – the last mill dates from the 1820s – the popular residential village is renowned for its dam and woodland, much of which was originally planted to supply pit props. The estate is now a country park embracing Kings Wood and Bushcliffe Wood. The Boathouse was built by William Pilkington of **CHEVET HALL** in the early 1800s as a sporting amenity and recently restored for public use.

NICHOLSON, WILLIAM

Prominent Wakefield printer and book publisher with works in Vicarage Street, Nicholson was born in 1835 in Halifax, his firm becoming a pioneer publishing house bringing cheap fiction to the masses together with hundreds of other titles 'in every department of literature, biography, history, poetry, travel and music.' He was very active in the public life of the city and became Chief Magistrate in 1891. His advocacy assisted the establishment of the West Riding County Council and **WAKEFIELD COUNTY HALL**. He died in 1901.

NICHOLSON, VIV
This ebullient **CASTLEFORD** miner's wife won £153,000 on the football pools in 1961 and famously announced she would 'Spend! Spend! Spend!' And she did, her profligacy sparking a stage play dramatising her spree.

NINETY-NINE ARCHES
Well-known architectural landmark that carries a railway line over the **CALDER RIVER** in Wakefield. The impressive structure is one of the longest in the country.

NIPSEY MONEY
Emergency allowances paid to wageless striking miners in pre-strike fund days, from pooled funds received either by donations or collections. On 18 September 1905, 2 shillings was awarded to each striking miner at the Hemsworth Colliery

NORMANTON
Part of the Kingdom of Elmet in the seventh century, the village was encompassed by an earthwork in Norman times, its original church of All Saints being administered by the Knights Hospitallers who resided nearby at **NEWLAND HALL**. Prominent Elizabethan barrister John Freeston endowed a grammar school used until 1887. Industrialisation radically altered the rural fabric of the village, the coming of the railway in 1840 leading to the creation of an important junction with a fine station – it was said to have stood within the moat of a Roman camp – and engine sheds, the manufacture of steel and the extraction of coal drawing workers from all parts of the UK and from Ireland. Mining recession has been alleviated in recent years by the creation of **WAKEFIELD EUROPORT**.

NORMANTON FORGE
Pioneering producer of steel established at a foundry on the eastern side of the railway around 1865. The forge specialised in steel-topped railway rails, the iron/steel-laminated construction offering extraordinary strength and flexibility. The works closed in 1879.

NORTHERN OLD BOYS' BOOK CLUB
Largely devoted to the works of Frank Richard, the creator of Billy Bunter, the club is appropriately run from an address in Thornes Road, Wakefield known as 'Greyfriars'.

NOSTELL
Historic village having its origins after the Battle of Winwidfield (also spelt

Winwood and Winwaed) in 655. King Oswy of Northumbria sought the intercession of a hermit in his fight with the heathen King Penda, promising to endow a monastery if victorious. The battle was won and Oswy was true to his word, the monastery becoming the Priory of St Oswald in the reign of Henry I. The estate was bought by prosperous silk merchants, the **WINN FAMILY** in 1654, their ownership continuing to this day. They mined coal in the village in the early nineteenth century and built colliery cottages known as Nostell Long Row. Nearby is the hamlet of Foulby where the famous inventor of the marine chronometer, John **HARRISON**, once lived.

NOSTELL PRIORY

Palladian National Trust mansion erected for the Winn family in 1733 to designs by James Paine on the site of a twelfth century Augustinian priory whose ruins were still extant in 1765 – fragments still remaining in outbuildings. The surveyor and historian Leland who visited the priory at its zenith reported: '...the building of this House is exceeding great and fair: and hath the goodlyest Fontein of Conduit Water that is yn that Quarter of England.' The successor mansion was extended by Robert Adam and furnished by Thomas Chippendale, the collection forming the finest suite of his furniture in existence.

Arms of Nostell Priory.
Extracted from *Old Yorkshire* edited by William Smith, 1884.

NOTTON

Rural village whose ancient manor was once a deer park. The village has five listed buildings including an old milestone and a railway bridge built by George Stephenson. In the wooded Notton Park are the remains of Iron Age workings.

NOTTON CUTTING

Excavations to accommodate the route of a local canal, created a massive hole that at the time was one of the largest in Great Britain.

NOWT ADDED AND NOWT TAKEN OUT

Famous advertising slogan of wholemeal flour producers **ALLINSON**, the allusion referring to the use of wholegrain cereals with no added ingredients.

O

ORANGERY, WAKEFIELD

Formerly a garden area in Back Lane belonging to prominent eighteenth century cloth manufacturer Pemberton **MILNES**. His daughter, the

Dowager Viscountess Galway who was a keen horticulturist, built the 1790s hothouse for tropical fruit cultivation, which was opened on a commercial basis in 1839 after her death. The building had a resident bear but the animal escaped and fatally mauled the keeper's wife. The building and grounds were presented to the adjacent **WAKEFIELD, WESTGATE CHAPEL** in 1850 and used for over a century for educational and recreational purposes, the garden providing extra burial space. The building was rescued from decay and refurbished for office use in the 1990s, Public Arts currently occupying the premises as their headquarters.

OSSETT

A town once dominated by its old nineteenth century stone mills when the processing of 'shoddy' and 'mungo' woollen wastes and the production of woollen machinery were major industries. **CUSSONS** soap has its origins in the town, which is now attractively pedestrianised around the Edwardian Town Hall. This building has its own restored theatre organ. **OSSETT SPA** promised to gentrify the town in the nineteenth century but the project folded.

OSSETT SPA

From early times, a spring on Low Common was noted for its efficacy, local stonemason James Ward recognising the commercial potential of the site in developing a medicinal spa in an era when mineral waters in Boston Spa and Harrogate were big business. In the early part of the nineteenth century, Ward is known to have built a suite of warm and cold baths, a contemporary description of his pioneering establishment surviving: 'The premises are delightfully situated and the waters have been analysed by several eminent men and spoken of by them as little inferior to Cheltenham: they have already gained a very high reputation for the many surprising cures they have performed. These water are celebrated for curing gout, rheumatism and the scrofula.' By 1826 a second baths had been erected and tenanted by a man called David Land, 'providing medicated vapour, sulphureous, sitting, shower and plunge baths with a separate establishment for the poor at a reduced price.' Speculation fever grew, and by 1879, there were grandiose reports in the *Ossett Observer* of developing a 'Little Harrogate.' Land for villas was bought, an architect was instructed and plots were laid out and planted with trees. One palatial mansion – Goring House – was built but the rest of the scheme foundered through lack of investment interest, only a single small circular stone ruin standing as a testimony to what might have been.

OUTWOOD

Now a suburb of Wakefield, the Out Wood was a pleasant tract of open country when local horse racing was transferred here in the latter half of the

Horse-drawn bus in Outwood. The John Goodchild Collection. Courtesy of www.twixtaireandcalder.org.uk; The online archive of Wakefield District Images

eighteenth century. The new course was properly laid out and provided with every modern amenity including paddocks and an elegant grandstand. Pictured in an illustration in Walker's *History of Wakefield and its People*, this red-bricked building became a farmhouse. It was blown up with explosives in 1924 after becoming unsafe. The racecourse utilised common land extending in total to some 2,500 acres alongside turnpike roads. This was enclosed under the Wakefield Inclosure Act of 1793, restrictions effectively ending horse racing in the district. Coal mining created the modern village, the construction of the **LAKE LOCK RAIL ROAD** adding to its prosperity in the nineteenth century.

P

PANCRACK

Local slang term for state-assisted unemployment benefit.

PANNELL, MARY

Infamous witch who lived in a cave in the Broc-o-dale area on the banks of the **WENT RIVER** near **WENTBRIDGE**. The remote locality once attracted 'covens of vile wretches, hags and sorcerers'. The lady is supposed to have bewitched to death William Witham of Ledston Hall to the north. She was tried and convicted of witchcraft at York and burned at the stake in 1603, her place of execution near Ledsham still being the name Mary Pannell Hill.

PARAGON BUSINESS VILLAGE
Key commercial development north of Wakefield at Snowhill. It has almost immediate access to Junction 41 of the M1.

PARKHILL COLLIERY
Situated in Wakefield, the pit was badly damaged by an underground fire on 29 October 1919. The local mines rescue service was called out and trapped miners were assisted to safety through an unaffected shaft. Surface damage was excessive and many men were thrown out of work. The mine eventually closed in 1982.

PERFECTS
Family of horticulturalists and seedsmen active in **PONTEFRACT** during the seventeenth century. They produced exotic plants shrubs and trees for landscaping schemes developed for large country houses, gardens and orangeries, gaining a reputation as the best nursery in Yorkshire. In the 1790s, they supplied seeds to the kitchen garden in Wentworth Woodhouse and trees to stock the deer park in the Studley Roger estate adjacent to Fountains Abbey. They also grew **LIQUORICE**. At the height of the firm's success, the directors upped roots and became bankers. By 1834, John and William Perfect were registered as bankers in Ropergate.

PETERSON, HENRY
American merchant who came to live in Wakefield in 1784, after developing a very successful business in Utrecht, Holland. He quit Holland following disturbances and toured England, commenting: 'In all I have seen of this happy isle, I preferred the little private town of Wakefield.' Peterson's son studied at the internationally regarded **WAKEFIELD QUEEN ELIZABETH'S GRAMMAR SCHOOL** and, with a sizeable investment from his father, joined a cloth making partnership with local manufacturer George Oxley. Peterson senior lived in Grove House in Kirkgate later commissioning a handsome new residence in Warrengate. The family name is honoured in the local street named Peterson Road.

PHANTOM OF OLD SNYDALE
Ghost of William Longthorne who was brutally murdered with a cut-throat

*Alsop's House.*LMA

razor in 1828 by William Mosey at Dole
Close, Old Snydale. Critically injured,
he crawled to Alsop's House – now the
Cross Keys public house – but died
shortly afterwards. In 1965, his blood
stained apparition a motorcyclist whose
waist was encircled by a weightless pillion-passenger, was seen by a lady, and
a bus driver and two of his passengers. The spirit was exorcised in 1966.

PILKINGTON, SIR JOHN

Born around 1425, one of the scions of a family who were eventually to reside
at **CHEVET HALL**, this **YORKIST** fought at the battle of **WAKEFIELD
GREEN** in 1460 but was captured and imprisoned in the Tower of London.
A financial opportunist, he became rich when the white rose bloomed,
although he was briefly interned in **PONTEFRACT CASTLE** in 1470. He
became a Crown Commissioner and an MP and developed estates in
Wakefield at Lupset Hall and Snapethorpe Hall. He also endowed a chantry
chapel in **WAKEFIELD CATHEDRAL**. He died in 1479.

PILKINGTON, LADY KATHLEEN

One of the Pilkington's of **CHEVET HALL**, this pioneering lady was instrumental in firmly establishing the French Bulldog as an English breed and helped found the Toy Bulldog Club. During the First World War, she ran a Red Cross Hospital for wounded soldiers in the hall at **DARRINGTON** and, after the hostilities, helped convert the premises for use as a medical centre for incurables.

PINDERFIELDS HOSPITAL

Large NHS Trust hospital in Wakefield with many specialised departments including a specialist county burns unit. In 1948, a hospital school was established to meet the educational needs of children under care.

PISSOIR

The only surviving example of the type of cast iron men's urinal made by the Saracen Foundry in Glasgow by the firm of MacFarlanes around 1880, is situated in front of a suburban bungalow in Front Street, Glasshoughton. Wakefield MDC proposed to move the rusting structure in 1994, but over 200 local residents petitioned for its preservation.

Pissoir in Glasshoughton, Castleford. LMA

PITCHFORK, ROLAND VIVIAN

Outstanding watercolorist born in Wakefield in 1895, Pitchfork attended **WAKEFIELD QUEEN ELIZABETH'S GRAMMAR SCHOOL** and studied at local art colleges before attending the Royal College of Art in 1921. His early canvases were inspired by the gritty Yorkshire landscape, later works showing influences by artists such as Braque, Cezanne, Derain and Picasso. He returned to his love of wilderness in his stirring compositions *Harlech Bay in a Storm* and *The Harbour at Borth-y-guent*. During the 1939-45 conflict, he became a war artist. A gifted painter, Pitchfork – 'Pitch' to his friends – became a Member of the Royal Academy in 1953. He died in 1982. A number of his paintings are on display in **WAKEFIELD ART GALLERY**.

PIT LASSES

In the first half of the nineteenth century, women and young children were routinely occupied in winning coal. Females and children were cheaper to employ than men and, driven by poverty, they were often prepared to endure the jobs that men regarded as overly demanding. Lashed to ropes, they would draw tubs of coal to the surface and would operate windlasses, one nineteen-year-old local girl complaining in 1854: 'Men do not like the winding. It's too hard for them.' Children would screen coal for rocks and would tediously operate ventilation doors underground, some women joining the men at the pit face to hew coal. Fuelled by sensational stories in the press, there was a national outcry for redress and a Royal Commission was set up to investigate the scandal, one West Riding Commissioner reporting thus: 'In many of the collieries there is no distinction of sex. The labour is distributed indifferently among both sexes, excepting that it is comparatively rare for the women to hew or get the coals, although there are numerous instances in which they regularly perform even this work. In great numbers of coal pits in the district men work in a state of perfect nakedness, and in this state are assisted in their labour by females of all ages, from girls of six years old to women of twenty one, these females being themselves quite naked down to the waist.' A surveyor was approached by one such pit lass with the lament: 'Oh Sir! This is sore work. I wish to God the first woman who tried to bear coals had broke her back and none would have tried it again.' After an indictment of the appalling conditions in the mines, Lord Shaftesbury's Mines Act of 1842 sought to 'prohibit the employment of women and girls in mines and collieries' but the abuses continued. In 1847, as nine-year-old Patience Wroe worked underground pushing tubs at the Caphouse Colliery at Overton (now the **NATIONAL COAL MINING MUSEUM FOR ENGLAND**), her hair was ignited by the stub of a candle. She was badly burnt and disfigured but she survived, her employer, with some conscience, appointing her to a domestic position in his own house.

PLAGUE STONE

Ancient hollowed-out receptacle for coins situated on the outskirts of **ACKWORTH**. It was probably last used by quarantined villagers in the plague of 1645 as a vinegar-filled sterilising bath for coins. These were collected by good Samaritans in payment for food. A register extract in Ackworth's St Cuthbert's Church reads: 'Richard Pickeringe and Ffrances Ledsoure – married June 25 1645 – in which year there dyed of the Plague in Ackworth 153 persons'.

Plague stone at Ackworth. LMA

POMFRET 60 LONGBOW TOURNAMENT

Annual autumn competition for archers in **PONTEFRACT**, marksmen competing with 60 arrows using targets set at 60 yards distance.

PONTEFRACT

An ancient citadel and market town built in the shadow of **PONTEFRACT CASTLE**. There is much debate about the origins of the name of this town of the 'broken bridge', the name having been spelt forty different ways in its long history. The name could refer to Bubwith Bridge, a crossing that once spanned a considerable stream. In the Middle Ages it was the main commercial centre of West Yorkshire. The town was noted for sand quarrying, cast iron manufacture, malting, tanning, motor engineering, coal

The ancient Counting House. LMA

Sessions House. LMA

*St Giles Parish Church, Pontefract.*LMA

mining but mainly for **PONTEFRACT RACECOURSE** and the production of **LIQUORICE**. The town had two permanent barracks for soldiers of the York and Lancaster Regiment and the **KING'S OWN YORKSHIRE LIGHT INFANTRY**. It boasts a number of architectural gems including the Town Hall, **PONTEFRACT BUTTERCROSS**, *The Red Lion Hotel*, the timber framed *Counting House* public house and the unusual **HERMITAGE**. In 1872, the town hosted the count of the first ever secret ballot in Great Britain, the returning officer sealing the ballot boxes with a **PONTEFRACT CAKE** hand stamp.

PONTEFRACT, ALL SAINTS

Originally the parish church, the dramatic ruin was badly damaged during the cannon exchanges between Parliamentarian and Royalist forces in the Civil War. It was partly repaired in 1838, although St Giles in the market place became the town's parish church in 1789.

PONTEFRACT BARCLAYS BANK

One of the oldest bank premises in the county

Ballot Box. Pontefract Museum

opened as Leatham, Tew and Company in 1801. One of its main shareholders was Thomas, William **TEW**.

PONTEFRACT BUTTERCROSS
Given to the town in 1734, this appealing little structure has rounded arches and a hipped roof and was originally used for selling market produce. It was built on the site of **PONTEFRACT SAINT OSWALD'S CROSS**.

PONTEFRACT CAKE
Confectionery disc of liquorice impressed with a trademark castle. First produced in 1760 by enterprising local chemist George Dunhill at the *Old Castle Inn*. Also known as **YORKSHIRE PENNIES**, the cakes were hand made by nimble-fingered ladies, who were expected to shape and stamp up to 25,000 cakes in a single 8-hour day.

PONTEFRACT CASTLE
Demolished on the orders of Parliament in 1649 (local residents petitioned to be allowed to recoup some of their war losses by selling off lead and stone) the castle was once one of the most impressive fortresses in Europe. Its power and scale can be imagined by examining the painting by Kierincx in **PONTEFRACT MUSEUM** and can be judged by a contemporary description written by a military man who inspected the citadel in 1634. 'In the circuit of this castle there are seven famous towers, of that amplitude as may entertain so many princes, as sometimes have commanded this island. The highest of them is called the Round Tower, in which that unfortunate Prince (Richard II) was enforced to flee round a post till his barbarous butchers inhumanely deprived him of life. Upon that post the cruel hackings and fierce blows doth still remain. We viewed the spacious hall, the large fire

Pontefract Castle. LMA

Pontefract Castle kitchens. LMA

kitchen which is long with many wide chimneys in it. Then we went up and saw the Chamber of Presence, the King and Queen's Chamber, the Chapel and many other rooms, all fit and suitable for princes. As we walked on the leads which cover the famous castle, we took a large and fair prospect of the country 20 miles about. York we there easily saw and plainly discovered to which place (after we had pleased the she-keeper, our guide) we thought fit to hasten...'. In the late Saxon and early medieval periods, the castle was strategically located, guarding the principal highway to the north and the route westwards crossing the **AIRE RIVER** to the Pennines. The 'Key to the North', the castle was a notorious and dreaded prison for political prisoners and was referred to by Shakespeare as 'Bloody Pomfret'. Richard II, the king, referred to in the 1634 description, perishing here in 1400:

> *Sometimes am I king;*
> *Then treason makes me wish myself a beggar,*
> *And so I am; then crushing penury*
> *Persuades me I was better when a king;*
> *Then am I kinged again, and by and by*
> *Think that I am unkinged by Bolingbroke,*
> *And straight am nothing.*

The castle was a Royalist stronghold during the Civil War and was besieged three times, the gallant defenders surviving bombardment and undermining. During the sieges they minted siege coins to help pay the garrison. The tale of local Royalist soldier John **MORRIS** is one of outstanding audacity, bravery and heroism. In Victorian times, the castle grounds were planted with trees and access improvements were completed in 1988 when a visitor centre was opened.

PONTEFRACT KING'S SCHOOL

The town has an educational heritage stretching back to monastic times, the origins of the famous King's School – one of the oldest in England- dating back to the 1139. It has been associated with the Duchy of Lancaster since 1588. The school had a disruptive history – it was reformed in 1563, 1583 and 1792 – and was established in the eighteenth century in Back Northgate near Cockpit Lane. It was sold in 1877 and was eventually destroyed by fire in 1902. After a gap of thirteen years and much local debate and fund raising, it was re-opened in an adapted military depot in Back Northgate in 1890, moving to its present site in Mill Hill in 1932. It produced two outstanding celebrities – John **BRAMALL** and Lord Martin Bladen **HAWKE**.

PONTEFRACT MUSEUM

Erected in red brick and visually arresting yellow terracotta in 1905, this attractive structure was once described by Poet Laureate Sir John Betjeman as one of the most beautiful Art Nouveau buildings in Yorkshire. Exhibits chart the history of the local **LIQUORICE** industry and there is a fine collection of siege coins minted to pay the troops during the three Civil war sieges. A seventeenth century painting shows the castle unmolested.

PONTEFRACT RACECOURSE

Racing was first recorded on the course in the 1720s. By the end of the eighteenth century, regular race days brought large crowds and a grandstand was erected in 1802 although this was pulled down by disgruntled investors in 1844. Steeple-chasing was revived and in 1879 a new stand was built, the

Pontefract Racecourse. Pontefract Museum

Pontefract Racecourse Grandstand. Pontefract Museum

course reaching the zenith of its popularity in 1957 when crowds of 15,000 spectators could be expected. Following improvements in 1983, the flat course became the longest in Europe.

PONTEFRACT SAINT OSWALD'S CROSS

This Christian totem, a focus of prayer and pilgrimage, stood on the site of the present **PONTEFRACT BUTTERCROSS**. It was dedicated to the sanctified warrior King Oswald, the ruler of Northumbria from 633 until his death in a battle with the pagan King Penda of Mercia in 641. The cross was probably erected in his memory, its immediate precincts being regarded as holy ground where fugitives could claim sanctuary, claiming freedom from arrest for debt and other offences. The cross became a focal point for meetings of officials from the local wapentake and a rendezvous point, traders congregating in its shadow to sell their wares. It is shown on a Civil War siege map, consisting of a shaft accessed by three steps from where proclamations would be read. The cross was probably mutilated by the Puritans but was repaired in 1671. Sadly, it was finally demolished, after standing for over a thousand years, in 1734, local antiquary Richard Gough lamenting its loss saying: '…as if Pontefract was to show no evidence of its splendour, St Oswald's Cross has given place these thirty years to an unmeaning market house', (the Buttercross).

POST MORTEM PATRIS PRO FILIO

After The Death Of The Father We Are For The Son – Pontefract's famous motto – a defiant vow of allegiance by the defenders of **PONTEFRACT CASTLE** upon the execution of Charles I.

POTTER, JOHN

Potter was born in Wakefield in 1674. His father owned a linen-drapers shop in the Market Place – now the **BLACK ROCK** public house. A talented scholar, he was educated at the local grammar school, distinguishing himself particularly in the study of Greek literature. He went on to matriculate at Oxford, wrote the first volume of his Antiquities of Greece in 1697 and took a degree of Doctor of Divinity soon afterwards. He had a distinguished ecclesiastical career culminating in his appointment as Archbishop of Canterbury at the age of sixty-four in 1737. He died in 1747 and is buried in the chancel of Croydon church.

POULSON, JOHN

PONTEFRACT - based architect who during the 1960s built up one of the largest practices in the UK. His bankrupt business collapsed in 1972 revealing mountains of debt including an outstanding tax bill of £688,000. An expose by Paul Foot in the investigative and satirical magazine *Private Eye* illuminated a scandalous web of bribery and intrigue and police were called in to investigate. Tainted by the sandal, former MP and Home Secretary Reginald Maudling resigned. Poulson was brought to trial in Leeds in 1974, the fifty-two day hearing – the longest trial for corruption in legal history – examining one hundred witnesses and over 500 documents. The proceedings cost an estimated £1.25 million. The accused famously said: 'I have never tried to bribe anybody' but he was found guilty of conspiracy to make or receive corrupt gifts. He admitted that

John Poulson. Pontefract Museum

cash and presents had been offered as inducements to secure contracts but denied corruption. The court heard that the sixty-three-year-old had given away more than £500,000 in suits, holidays and flowers to win favours, the Leader of Newcastle Council – T Dan Smith receiving a fee of £155,000. Poulson was found guilty of corruption and sentenced to five years. Donald Herrod QC commented: 'He has nothing to live for and his abiding fear is that he will never complete this sentence because of his ill health.' In Leeds gaol, he made a confession, pleading guilty to nine charges of corruption and conspiracy, the trial judge increasing his sentence by two years. Poulson's corrosive web enmeshed some twenty-three local authorities and around three hundred individuals, MP's, police officers, members of health authorities and civil servants all coming under his influence. Many of the guilty parties were never brought to justice. Before he died in 1993, Poulson published his memoirs in a book – *The Price*.

PUGNEYS

Country park established in the 1970s off the Denby Dale Road near Wakefield, offering windsurfing, dingy sailing, canoeing and power-boating on a large lake utilising land formerly used for quarrying. The park has a miniature railway – the Pugneys Light Railway – open at weekends and on bank holidays.

PYRAMIDAL LODGE

Ornamental Tuscan columned and pedimented pyramid-shaped gateway to **NOSTELL PRIORY** known locally as the **NEEDLE'S EYE**.

Q

QUAKERS

Adherents to a religious sect called the Society of Friends, a creed having no regular ministry or definite creed. The body was formed by George Fox who began a preaching tour in 1647. In 1651, he visited Wakefield but his harangues had little effect on the populace. During the following year, he tried again but his preaching again fell on largely hostile ears and he was threatened with the stocks. The sect was persecuted although several local families adopted the religion, which began to flourish. About 1695, they bought a plot of land in Doncaster Road for use as a burial ground. The denomination took its name from Fox's reference: 'to trembling at the name of the Lord.' One notable local Quaker was Luke **HOWARD** although he left the sect in 1836.

R

RADCLIFFE, JOHN

A distinguished physician, the son of a comfortable Yorkshire yeoman, Radcliffe was born near Wakefield in 1650. He rose to prominence at Court after residing and practising in Oxford for some years, his pioneering prescription of 'fresh air and exercise, generous nourishment and the use of cordials' bringing him into conflict with rival doctors. A loveable wag and eccentric he was much devoted to the 'purple God of the tavern.' On one occasion he was regaling his cup when a desperate, breathless and muscular husband entered the inn and implored: 'Doctor! My wife is at the point of death! Make haste. Come with me.' 'I will', replied the doctor leisurely, 'but not until I've finished the bottle.' With this, the desperate man snatched up the doctor in his arms and took him writhing from the tavern. 'Put me down!' Radcliffe insisted regaining the use of his legs. 'Now, you rascal. Yes, I'll cure your wife ... but I'll do it in revenge!' And he did. Radcliffe died in 1714.

RAILWAYS

In this super-hot technological age, we can send a probe to Mars and, if the train's not too late, we can speed through Wakefield District at light speed; although you will be allowed only one stop...in Wakefield. If you want to visit

Sandal and Walton Station. The John Goodchild Collection. Courtesy of www.twixtaireandcalder.org.uk: online archive of Wakefield District Images

anywhere else in the district, you have to jump. But it was not always so. Judging from *The West Riding of Yorkshire* by Bernard Hobson published in 1921, our grandparents were well served. He refers to the 'Midland and North-Eastern Swinton and Knottingley Line' the 'Knottingley to Burton Salmon Branch', the 'Great Northern Railway to Wakefield and Ossett', the 'Midland Line to Normanton', the 'Lancashire and Yorkshire Railway from Wakefield to Pontefract and Knottingley' and the 'Horbury Branch.' The bad old days?

READER, DOCTOR JEREMIAH

This able physician took over the practice at Westgate End House in 1888 (Robert Lawson **TAIT** was there in 1870). He was an extremely hard working doctor who held three surgeries every day apart from Sunday when there was only one afternoon consultation. Holidays were unknown. He would be roused at night with a loud knock, his groom having to spring from his bed to ready the horse and trap. On the doctor's return, the groom was expected to prepare the horse and vehicle for the next emergency. The eminent doctor made up his own medicines, carefully weighing each ingredient and bottling each prescription before affixing a hand written label and wrapping up the medicine with his own hand. He charged 3 shillings and 6 pence for a home visit and 15 shillings for attending a confinement. In the 1890s the unfortunate Reader was bitten by a rabid pet dog. He was not expected to survive but he pluckily cauterised the bite in a solution of carbolic and left immediately for Paris to see the only man in the world who could save his life – the legendary Louis Pasteur. Reader's son recorded his father's brave fight: 'As my father never went anywhere and had never been abroad, this was a most sensational step for him to take. He had two week's treatment. Every day except Sunday he was held in a grip of iron by an enormously strong male attendant. A large needle and a huge syringe were used, and from 10 ml to 20 ml of vaccine were injected into his abdominal wall.' The doctor pulled through and eventually died in 1918, his son continuing the grand medical tradition.

REDOUBT

The first licensed premise on the **WESTGATE RUN** in Wakefield. The 200 year old pub was originally known as the *Spotted Cow*, a new landlord – a Coldstream Guard veteran – renaming it in 1882 in honour of comrades who stormed a fortress called the Great Redoubt during the Crimean War.

REEF

Two hundred million years ago, the Wakefield district was covered by a shallow tropical sea. An exposed cliff in a quarry in **SOUTH ELMSALL** reveals fossilised remains of sea creatures that once thrived in the area.

REEVE, RICHARD (RESTORATION LTD)

Specialist valuable book and document conservation and repair service situated in **CROFTON**. The firm is dedicated to keeping the art of hand bookbinding alive.

RHODES, JOHN

A shrewd and opportunistic rags-to-riches mining speculator who allegedly came to **PONTEFRACT** as a consequence of reading a report in the *Illustrated London News* about gas burning on water in **FEATHERSTONE** in 1872. A former factory hand, he had no expertise in geology but the signs persuaded him sink a new pit on open parkland north of the town, the Prince of Wales Colliery becoming one of the most productive in the area. A blunt and cussed Yorkshireman in the grand tradition, he never warmed to trade unionism or to the strange notion of holidays. On one famous occasion he was asked by an employee for a few days leave. Nonplussed, he replied: 'Why lad is tha badly?' The miner responded affirming his good health, Rhodes countering with: 'Well, when you're badly you're best at home, and when you're well, you're best at work!'

Rhodes lived in luxury in Snydale Hall and became Lord Mayor of Pontefract a record nine times. When he died in 1911, his pit was a vast concern employing 1452 men. He left an estate valued at £540,626.

RHUBARB

Speciality early season vegetable, grown in forcing sheds in the Rhubarb Triangle between Lofthouse, East **ARDSLEY, STANLEY** and Morley in Leeds. From the late 1870s until the mid twentieth century, trains hauled between 80-100 tons each trip to Covent Garden Market in London and a reduced but still lucrative trade continues by road. Some of the produce is exported to France for use in the production of champagne and it is also used to flavour beer and a local ewes milk cheese called Ruby Gold sold in specialist shops in Wakefield and **CASTLEFORD**. Wakefield hosts a

Rhubarb by candlelight, E Oldroyd and Sons. WMDC

Festival of Rhubarb – tours of forcing sheds and themed lunches – every year. 'There's nothing more romantic than holding hands with someone in a Wakefield forcing shed and listening to the ruby red rhubarb grow. All this by candlelight.' (Anonymous) Children would once play in the rhubarb fields and would break off the 'dolly knocker seed sticks' to use as clubs!

RIDDINGS DRIFT MINE
Sunk in 1970, the **SOUTH KIRKBY** mine achieved a British productivity record of over 18 tons a man/shift during the week ending March 27 1971.

RIDINGS CENTRE, WAKEFIELD
Flagship retail shopping complex in the centre of Wakefield, three tiered malls offering 90 quality shops, radiating from an atrium and food courtyard. The centre has over 100 integral car parking spaces.

ROAD MENDING
In the seventeenth century, all householders were obliged by law to labour, without recompense, for six days each year in repairing local roads. Horse and carts were also to be provided free. These impositions caused much shirking and dispute. In 1641 three men from **STANLEY** were brought before the justices because 'they did not work for the repair of the King's highway within the township of Stanley for the space of five days as required by the overseer of the King's highways.' And in 1693 in Wakefield, the justices ordered '...that for the future, the inhabitants of Westgate, Northgate and Kirkgate repair the highways belonging to each street, distinctly by themselves, according to ancient custom.'

ROBBERY AND MURDER
A barbaric crime committed by six men and one woman in an undisclosed village near Wakefield in December 1677 was the subject of an eight-page pamphlet published in London shortly after the event. The crime was described as 'the most horridest and wickedest robbery and murder that hath ever been heard of for many years.' It was perpetrated on the Wilson family, the masked assailants breaking into their house and binding and gagging everyone inside. Anthony Wilson and his wife were tortured – a flame was held to the husband's fingers 'until such time as it had burned all the flesh from the bone' – in an attempt to discover a perceived cache of money, Anthony insisting that he only had six pounds in the house. After stealing everything of value, the robbers were ready to make their escape but the female insisted that everyone in the house be killed in order to stop them from testifying. The six men resisted the call, the woman snatching up a knife

and plunging it into Anthony's stomach. All seven made their escapes and Anthony Wilson died. According to the pamphlet, no arrests were ever made although years on, there was some suggestion that the atrocity had been perpetrated by the gang of William **NEVISON** who was executed at York in the following year. He was known to consort with five males and one female associate – Elizabeth Burton – who gave evidence at his trial but failed to mention the fatal stabbing of Wilson. Was she the murderer?

ROGERTHORPE MANOR
Famous as the alleged one time home of traitor William Joyce ('**LORD HAW HAW**' – the voice of 'Germany Calling'), the manor was built around 1600 probably on the site of a medieval settlement. It is reputed to be haunted by a phantom Cavalier who stalks the rooms by moonlight and also by a mischievous Victorian child who opens cupboards and rattles doors. The manor is now a fashionable hotel.

ROSSE, EARLS OF
Pioneers in astronomy and the early development of the telescope. They lived at Womersley Hall and Birr Castle in Ireland. In 1845, the earl built an instrument that remained the largest in the world for seventy years. The family gave their name to the **ROSSE OBSERVATORY**.

ROSSE OBSERVATORY
Constructed and assembled by members of the **WEST YORKSHIRE ASTRONOMICAL SOCIETY** in 1983 and opened by personality astronomer Patrick Moore, the observatory is the world's first such amateur facility built for people with disabilities. It is equipped with sophisticated telescopes, reflectors and ancillary equipment and is open to members and visitors every night of the year.

ROYGBIV
Mnemonic remembered by generations of Yorkshire school children, an allusion to the temporary success of the duke at the Battle of **WAKEFIELD GREEN** – Richard Of York Gained Battle In Vain – the emboldened letters giving us the colours of the rainbow – red, orange, yellow, green, blue, indigo and violet.

ROYAL VISITS
As the administrative capital of the **WEST RIDING**, Wakefield has been frequently graced by visits from the royal family. In 1891, Prince Albert came to the city and opened the extension to the college of art. (In 1911, a massive bonfire that consumed over 100 tons of wood was burnt to celebrate the

Unveiling of the statue of Queen Victoria in Wakefield Bull Ring. LMA

coronation of King George V). Princess Elizabeth (the present queen) visited **PINDERFIELDS HOSPITAL** in 1945 and she came to Wakefield again with her husband in the Jubilee Year of 1977. Queen Elizabeth (the late Queen Mother) honoured Wakefield in 1947 and 1976 and in 1988, she visited **NOSTELL PRIORY**. The Prince and Princes of Wales made a historic journey to the city in 1985.

A modern view of the statue of Queen Victoria in Wakefield Bull Ring. LMA

RUGBY LEAGUE

Premier leisure occupation in Wakefield district at both amateur and professional levels, local teams **CASTLEFORD TIGERS, FEATHERSTONE ROVERS** and **WAKEFIELD TRINITY WILDCATS** helping to establish and popularise the game in the north of England. 'It's more than a game, it's a belief, a way of life', asserts the foreword to a definitive book on the subject *When Push Comes to Shove* by Ian **CLAYTON** and Michael Steele. The book bursts with anecdotes and photographs straight from the scrum: There is a story about a former Great Britain international second row forward who performed remarkable feats with his manhood, secreting a good jingle-full of old pennies under his foreskin. And there is another about a warning given by a phalanx of heavyweight forwards to a newly bloodied player who weighed a mere twelve stones. He was urged to 'look after himself' this coming from players who looked as if they had been 'whacked across the mush with a shovel.'

RYHILL

Until the early 1800s, the 'hill where rye was grown' was just a hamlet, the exploitation of locally discovered coal seams creating a colliery village served by a two railway lines and a widened Barnsley Canal. High-class clothing was manufactured in the village from 1966 until 1987, the 1972 British Olympic Team wearing Ryhill uniforms. Post mining recession, the village has made a good recovery.

S

SAINT AUSTIN ROMAN CATHOLIC CHURCH

On Margaret Street in Wakefield, this imposing church, in a surprisingly quiet neighbourhood close to the centre, was extended by the architect Joseph Aloysius Hansom between 1878 and 1879. He provided a new chancel, Lady Chapel, baptistery, sacristy and porch. The York architect is best known for his invention of the Hansom Cab.

SAINT JOHN THE BAPTIST CHAPEL

One of Wakefield's four chantry chapels, this building, on the site in Northgate now occupied by **WAKEFIELD QUEEN ELIZABETH'S GRAMMAR SCHOOL,** was founded in the thirteenth century and used as a parish church while the parish church was being rebuilt in the fourteenth century.

SAINT MARY MAGDALENE CHAPEL

The medieval chapel, which once stood on a triangular plot of land surrounded by a wall, was near the Ings Beck at the bottom of Westgate in Wakefield. A quaint, timber framed building with a stone roof and two bells, it was built mainly to accommodate plague victims to ensure that churchgoers in the parish church remained unafflicted. The building was once owned by the family of George **SAVILE** and was used for a time as a wool shop before its demolition around 1750.

SAINT SWITHIN'S CHAPEL
First mentioned in 1284, the chantry stood near **CLARKE HALL** beside a footpath that led to a ford over the **CALDER RIVER**. One of its stones found its way into a wall of St Swithin's Church on the Eastmoor Estate.

SAINTS' DAYS
In the days before annual calendars and morning newspapers, the inhabitants of Wakefield were reminded of the need to attend the parish church on saints days by the ringing of an extra bell. The practice was to ring one bell for five minutes at eight o'clock every morning on non-saint days. On saints' days, two bells were rung.

SALT, SIR TITUS
Textile entrepreneur, philanthropist and developer of the model village of Saltaire who served his first apprenticeship in premises in King Street, Wakefield having been educated in Enoch Harrison's academy in George Street.

SANDAL CASTLE
The finest excavated motte and bailey castle in Europe with twelfth century origins set on a sandstone ridge overlooking the **CALDER RIVER**. An administrative centre for the Manor of Wakefield, the castle was magnificently rebuilt in

Sir Titus Salt.
Extracted from *Yorkshire Greats*, William Smith, 1882.

stone in the thirteenth century and became a royal stronghold, Richard III intending to make the fortress his permanent base before his defeat at the Battle of Bosworth in 1485. During the **WARS OF THE ROSES** in 1460, Richard Duke of York was killed at the Battle of **WAKEFIELD GREEN**, the bloody contest being fought within sight of the castle walls. The structure slowly fell into disrepair until it was briefly refortified by Royalists during the Civil War. Parliament ordered that it be stripped of its defences in 1646. The site was extensively excavated between 1964 and 1973, discoveries forming the basis of a visitor and interactive exhibition centre.

SANDAL MAGNA
Village suburb south of Wakefield famous for its castle and its associations

with the Battle of **WAKEFIELD GREEN**. Its church of St Helen, dating from the 13th century, was the incumbency of Henry **ZOUCH**. The church has a number of treasures including cast-iron ledger plates to members of the Beaumont family and a chair used by William **NEVISON**.

SAVILE, GEORGE

A resident of Wakefield's Haselden Hall, (this gabled 17th century mansion in Northgate was demolished) Savile was a local benefactor whose legacy helped fund the erection of **WAKEFIELD PRISON**. His family once owned the chapel of **SAINT MARY MAGDALENE**.

SAVILE, SIR JOHN

This noble gentleman from Lupset, Wakefield, was a family relation of the owner of Howley Hall situated between Morley and Batley. During the Civil War, he was left in charge of the hall which was besieged by the Royalist Duke of Newcastle. He insisted that the property be handed over to his troops in the king's name. Sir John refused and, with small arms fire, managed to repel the intruders for a few days. The duke brought up cannon and blasted the hall to ruins and he looted its contents and killed most of the defenders. A valiant gamekeeper eventually opened the door to the assailants but he was brutally hacked to pieces and Sir John was taken prisoner and incarcerated in **PONTEFRACT CASTLE**. The Howley Hall estate is now a golf course. In recent years, several golfers have reported seeing strange spectres drifting over the links.

SAW INN

Long-demolished prominent and prestigious old inn on Westgate, Wakefield, its curtilage encompassing gardens, garths and horticultural land abutting Ings Lane. In 1792, its landlord had his own pew in the local church!

·SAW - INN, Wakefield.

TO BE SOLD,

(By *Auction*)

At the SAW - INN, in Wakefield,

On the 3d of May 1792,

Betwixt the Hours of 6 and 8 in the Evening,

(Unless before difpofed of by Private Contract) fubject to Conditions,

ALL that Freehold MESSUAGE, TENEMENT, or INN, known by the Sign of the SAW, ftanding on the South-fide of *Weftgate*, the principal Street in *Wakefield*, near the Centre of the Town, and now occupied by Mr. *Thomas Burnill*; together with the Cottages, Out-buildings, Garths, and Folds, thereto belonging ; and all thofe Pieces or Parcels of LAND, extending from the faid Inn, to the *Ings-Lane* there, occupied as Gardens, by feveral Perfons as Undertenants to the faid *Thomas Burnill*, and all Rights and Appurtenances belonging to, and now occupied with, the Premifes.

The LAND, divided into Gardens, ftands in a moft eligible Situation for building upon, and might be formed into an entire Street, to communicate from the Top of Weftgate to the Ings-lane. There is a good Pew in *Wakefield Church* belonging the Premifes.

The Tenant will fhew the Premifes ; and other Particulars may be had of Mr. SCOTT, Upholfterer, or of Mr. COLVARD, , Attorney at Law, both in *Wakefield*

*Saw Inn auction advertisement, 1792.*LM

SAYWELL, REVEREND JOSEPH LEMUEL

Incumbent at **ACKWORTH** from 1884 until 1887, this noted author produced a number of Yorkshire studies including *The Parochial History of*

Ackworth, the *History and Annals of Northallerton* and a number of religious tracts. His incendiary work *Cremation Negatively Considered* is now a highly sought-after novelty at specialist book fairs.

SCARGILL, ARTHUR

'King Arthur' was the President of the National Union of Mineworkers at the time of the memorable conflict with the Thatcher government during the Miners' **STRIKE** of 1984/85. He was born in 1938 into a mining family. His father, both his grandfathers' and all his male relatives were miners. He left school at fifteen in 1953 and began working at Woolley Colliery where he stayed for nineteen years. In 1961, he was elected as a member of the **WOOLLEY** branch of the NUM. He rose through the ranks as a left-wing activist, finally becoming President of the organisation in 1981. He left the Labour Party in 1996 to establish the Socialist Labour Party. A man who can generate fanatical loyalty and opprobrium in equal measure, he is the author of several publications including a history of the 1893 **FEATHERSONE MASSACRE**.

President Arthur Scargill pays tribute to miners who lost their lives in strikes at the annual ceremony, NUM headquarters, Barnsley, March 2002. Brian Elliott Collection

SEAL, SAMUEL

Nineteenth century quarry owner with commercial interests in **ACKWORTH,** Heath and **NORMANTON**. He settled in Wakefield in 1836 and quickly developed his expertise in quarrying, a growing fortune enabling him to build a villa – Stoneleigh House – in Doncaster Road in 1861. He erected the adjoining Stoneleigh Terrace a few years later, offering the properties for rent, the widow of Thomas **GISSING** relocating here in 1870. Her novelist son, George **GISSING** visited the house, his sojourns colouring chapters in his novel *A Life's Morning.*

SECKAR WOOD
One of only five Sites of Special Scientific Interest in the district, the wood was originally part of the **WOOLLEY HALL** estate. Its woodland, interspersed with wet and dry heathland, provides a habitat for rare plants.

SELBY CANAL
Waterway northeast of **KNOTTINGLEY** running for just over five miles, linking the **AIRE RIVER** with the inland port of Goole. It was needed because the river east of Haddesley to the Ouse was prone to summer droughts and winter floods, carriers requiring a more reliable artery. The canal was opened in 1778.

SERMONS ON THE MOUNT
Before the church of St Andrew's was opened for worship in 1846, the residents of Wakefield's Marsh Way area – it had a godless reputation as a place of moral and spiritual destitution – had to make do with a makeshift church located in a cottage 'next to Hampshire's shop.' The property was ill-designed for the purpose and great difficulty was experienced in installing a pulpit, its mountainous height only being accommodated by punching a hole in the cottage's parlour ceiling. During sermons, only half of the minister was visible but with a little contortionist climbing and crouching, the agile fellow did have the advantage of being able to address congregations in two rooms simultaneously.

SEWAGE
Until the age of enlightenment, most of Wakefield's effluvia poured into the stinking **CALDER RIVER** through flushless sewers. Passers-by resorted to two immediate expedients – the pearl divers breath and the clothes peg. According to an 1852 Board of Health Inquiry into public health in the town, the privies 'are never flushed by artificial means; when necessary they are cleansed by manual labour. No use is made of the sewage; it is allowed to run to waste in the Calder.' So bad were the nauseous stench and the condition of the grossly polluted river, that in 1866 a complainant wrote in perfectly legible script to Sir Robert Rawlinson's River Commission, having filled his inkwell at Wakefield Bridge!

SHAMBLES AND PUDDING MIDDENS
The market town of **PONTEFRACT** was once famous throughout the county for its meat, hundreds of beasts being slaughtered and presented for sale every week. The meat was displayed on stalls known as shambles, discarded guts, severed heads and limbs, referred to collectively as pudding,

going to middens behind the rows of medieval shops. The muck, mire and stench were tolerated for centuries until calls were made for a properly built meat market. This was opened by the Prime Minister Lord Palmerston in 1860. It was accommodated in an elegant building with fine exterior carvings showing the town's coat of arms and reliefs of animals and poultry. But it was unsuitable for its purpose. Gloomy and ill-

Façade of Pontefract Market Hall. LMA

ventilated, it drew a host of enduring criticism from the butchers and was finally demolished in 1957 only its grand façade surviving.

SHARLSTON

Former mining community individually comprised of Old Sharlston, New Sharlston and Sharlston Common. New Sharlston was created to accommodate miners who worked at Sharlston Colliery which opened in 1865. The village produced a phalanx of exceptional rugby league players including the famous Fox trio – Peter, Don and Neil – and Jonty Parkin.

SHARLSTON HALL

Four hundred years and the presence of intensive coal mining have done little to preserve the blithe spirit of Sharlston Hall. And yet, despite its antiquity and the surrounding industrialisation, the old hall emits a timeless romance, the story of a widow who was rescued from an intense period of mourning by love, still stirring the heart. The lady lost her beloved husband Richard Beaumont in 1704 and spent three years in cloistered grief at the hall never venturing far from its door. One day, two anxious horsemen passed by, one of the riders urgently seeking help for his friend who was in the grip of a serious fever. The widow offered her hospitality and, temporarily putting aside her own melancholy, she nursed the stranger back to health. Sufficiently recovered after three weeks, the gentleman caught a glimpse of the still lamenting widow in a window and became immediately smitten. He spoke of his feelings and within a short while, the widow recovered her zest for life. The couple were soon married, none other than the Earl of Westmorland taking possession of his happy bride and a revitalised Sharlston Hall which was soon reunited with its old reputation for laughter and song. For almost 150 years until 1851, the Westmorland family figured prominently in the mining fortunes of the village. In the nineteenth century, local MP W H Leatham wrote a ballad celebrating the halls romantic tale:

> *Old Sharlston Hall again was gay,*
> *With sound of minstrelsy,*
> *And the widow's voice arose once more*
> *Amidst the mirth and glee.*
>
> *Rightly goodly steeds were heard to neigh*
> *Within the widow's stalls,*
> *And faith! there was passing to and fro*
> *Amid the ancient halls!*
>
> *The turret-clock, that ne'er had ticked*
> *For many a silent year,*
> *Now scarcely could travel fast enough*
> *For peasant and for peer.*
>
> *For there was roasting on the spit,*
> *And frying o'er the fire,*
> *And the handing round of brimming cups*
> *By yeoman and by squire!*
>
> *And Apthorpe grooms with Sharlston maids*
> *Were dancing up and down,*
> *Till Sharlston Green was a fairy scene,*
> *All peopled like a town.*

SHARP, SAMUEL

Outspoken and sometimes prickly incumbent of **WAKEFIELD VICARAGE** from 1810 until his death at the advanced age of eighty-two in 1855. He was keenly involved in local education and charitable and hospital affairs, founding the Bell School in 1813 and a school for girls in Almshouse Lane a few years later. In his latter years, Sharp sank into debt – he invested in buying out a tailor's shop that had demeaned **CHANTRY BRIDGE CHAPEL WAKEFIELD** – and he had a public fallout with his curate. Sharp was evicted from the vicarage and his furniture was sold at auction. The curate was the subject of a supporting petition by one hundred and five parishioners who discreetly made reference to Sharp's 'infirmity of temper so frequently inseparable from old age.' But the curate was forced to resign. The geriatric Sharp died in 1855, the *Wakefield Journal* giving him a rather circumlocutory send off: 'His unflinching discharge of what he conceived to be his duty was perhaps his most conspicuous characteristic. No promise of popularity, no fear of obloquy, could seduce or deter him from maintaining any principle which he considered it to be his duty to uphold. And although such inflexibility of purpose must have at times an aspect of harshness, the event usually proves, as in this case, that a course of conduct uniformly directed by a sense of duty is one which none but a truly conscientious man can maintain.' The paper could have saved several column inches by quoting one member of his flock who said: 'He was a cantankerous old bugger who was always bloody well right!'

SHARPLES, JAMES

A Wakefield native, one of thirteen children born in 1825, he was the son of an iron founder who removed the family to Bury to follow his profession. He was largely illiterate but showed some early artistic talent by drawing images of his father's steam boilers on the kitchen floor. He went on to become a respected painter and an engraver.

SHAW, WILLIAM

Railway contractor and architect, famed for his tunnelling and excavation skills. Locally, he engineered the railway tunnels at Chevet and **WOOLLEY**, his contracts earning him a fortune. He designed the almshouses sponsored by Caleb **CROWTHER** and, against strong bidding, bought the Stanley Hall estate at auction in 1854. He died in 1862 and was buried in Wakefield Cemetery underneath a ridiculously ostentatious and pretentious monument capped with a spire. Local stonemason John Rogers slipped off a ladder to his death while he was working on the monument, 'nearly the whole of the stonemasons of the town following the corpse to the grave'.

SHELTON, THEOPHILUS

Architect who in 1694 bought an estate in Heath, building Eshald House for his own occupation. This was subsequently absorbed into **HEATH HALL**. He may have drawn up plans for Lupset Hall and **ALVERTHORPE HALL**. Shelton designed market crosses for Wakefield in 1707 (demolished in 1866) and Beverley in 1714, the latter cross still surviving.

SHEPHERD, AMBROSE

Born in 1855, he became an extensive landowner in the **CASTLEFORD** and **BADSWORTH** areas. A local character with a warm and generous heart, he became landlord of Castleford's *Garden House Inn* in 1880. His generosity to good causes, including a donation to help homeless families displaced by the explosion at **HICKSON AND WELCH** in 1930, was legendary. In 1930, he gave £500 to Castleford and Normanton District Hospital. He became a well-to-do resident of Blackpool and died there in 1943.

SHERWOOD, BENJAMIN
Wakefield publican, hotelier and theatre proprietor who ran a music hall at the *Crown and Anchor* in Kirkgate under the successive names *The People's Music Hall* and the *Gaiety*. The impresario bought the old Wakefield theatre in 1883 but its age and decrepitude thwarted commercial success, the council recognising its fire hazards and refusing to renew its licence in 1892. Sherwood boldly commissioned Frank Matcham, the most successful theatre architect of the day, to design the **WAKEFIELD OPERA HOUSE** whose curtain first rose on 15 October 1894. Sherwood left his wife and quit Wakefield in 1900 for Old Colwyn in Wales.

SHIPMAN, HAROLD
Medical practitioner responsible for the murder of at least 215 patients by lethal injection. Convicted in January 2000 and sentenced to fifteen life terms, he was transferred to **WAKEFIELD PRISON** in June 2003, the Category A prisoner committing suicide on 13 January 2003 by hanging himself from his cell bars with knotted bed sheets. A regular drug user, he was employed from 1970 until 1974 as a houseman at Pontefract General Infirmary and may, according to the sixth report of the official inquiry into the deaths, have unlawfully killed a further 137 patients during his training. Notes made after a meeting with police investigators and Home Office inspectors prior to his trial record: 'He stated that he had acquired this preference (for pethidine) whilst working as a doctor at a hospital in **PONTEFRACT**.

SILCOATES SCHOOL
Founded in 1809 as the Yorkshire Protestant Dissenters Grammar School utilising Silcoates Hall. The school was closed within ten years but was revived in 1831, pupils of the time existing on a diet of bread and milk for breakfast, meat and plain pudding for dinner and bread and milk for supper. The building caught fire during the Easter holidays in 1910 – the pupils were absent on vacation – and the fire brigade was summoned. As **WRENTHORPE** was outside the city boundaries, the Wakefield appliances could not attend. By the time the Dewsbury brigade turned up, it was too late! The independent school was reopened in 1908, its modern facilities including a magnificent science and technology block, a swimming pool and a sports field all set in fifty-five acres.

SILKSTONE ROW
Part of a largely demolished collection of colliers' housing known collectively as 'The Buildings' in **ALTOFTS**, the properties reputedly formed the

Silkstone Row, Altofts. Brian Elliott Collection

longest row of three-storey terraced cottages in Europe being part of one of the oldest planned coalfield settlements in the West Riding Coalfield. The development provided integrated workers, mine officials and mine managers houses, a school with a headmaster's house, a cooperative store and a Wesleyan chapel. The comprehensive scheme, executed in the 1850s, even included allotment gardens and a recreation ground.

SIMPSON, EDWARD

The son of a working man who made a fortune manufacturing soap, Simpson was classically educated at Harrow and Oxford. He took over his father's business and became a country gentleman with a passion for riding to hounds and entertaining. A grandee with high ambitions and expensive tastes, he bought **WALTON HALL** for £114,000 in 1878 from the heir of Charles **WATERTON**. His purchase enabled him to settle a long festering dispute between his father and the old squire whose complaints about the stink from the soap works caused it to be relocated to a site in Thornes in the early 1850s. But the hall had a determined sitting tenant, his implacability lasting until his death in 1891 when Simpson finally moved into the mansion. In 1906, the failing soap business was sold to Lever Brothers and the works were closed. Financially broken, Simpson died in 1914.

SIRDAR
Prominent yarn and carpet company founded in 1880 with mills at **ALVERTHORPE** and **OSSETT** employing around 500 people.

SIX CHIMNEYS
This quaintly gabled but rickety multi-hearthed old property built in1566 was a local landmark in Wakefield. It was a shop for many years but it was allowed to finally collapse in 1941. A number of drawings and paintings of the building survive. According to legend, the house was haunted by a ghost called Lady Margaret, who starved herself to death after someone locked her in one of the cramped attic rooms.

Clean Sweep. LMA

The 'Six Chimneys', Kirkgate, Wakefield. Cultural Services, City Engineers Collection. Courtesy of www.twixtaireandcalder.org.uk: The online archive of Wakfied District Images

SMART, SIR JACK:
Born in **ALTOFTS** in 1920, this former miner became a trade union official, a local magistrate and the leader of the council. His civic achievements were recognised in the award of a CBE and in 1985, he joined the ranks of the **HONORARY FREEMAN OF WAKEFIELD**.

SMEATON, JOHN
Eminent Leeds civil engineer and member of the Royal Society with a particular expertise in constructing canals, harbours and mills. He pioneered the use of dovetailed blocks of Portland Stone and hydraulic lime during his reconstruction of the Eddystone Lighthouse and was the Chief Engineer for the **AIRE AND CALDER NAVIGATION** between 1757 and 1763.

SNAP
Colloquial term for a packed lunch with allusions to a snatched mouthful.

SOMERVILLE, JAMES
This friend to Pontefract's pub crawling fraternity, created a map in 1952 showing the location of all the town's pubs and clubs using the famous format devised for the London Underground.

SORBY, THOMAS CHARLES
Architect born at Chevet, near Wakefield. He went to work in London and won a design competition for Bromley Town Hall. In 1885 he left England for Canada and designed the Glacier House Hotel and railway stations at Peterborough and Yorkville all for the Canadian Pacific Railway. He also designed the Bank of British Columbia and the Court House in Vancouver.

SOUTH ELMSALL
A former mining town whose **FRICKLEY COLLIERY** provided sustained employment for nearly a century. It has a **BRASS BAND**. The Royalist hero Colonel John **MORRIS** lived in Hague Hall.

SOUTH KIRKBY
Sister former mining community to **SOUTH ELMSALL**. Overlooking Brierley Common is an oval prehistoric earthwork rising to 300 feet and covering nearly five acres with cliffs on the northern and southern flanks. Its earthen ramparts are still ten feet high in places.

SPANISH ARMADA
Men of the district were mobilised to counter the threatened Spanish invasion in 1588. Four hundred soldiers from the wapentakes of Agbrigg

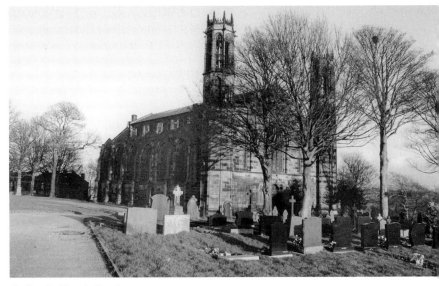

St Peter's Church, Stanley. LMA

(which included the town of Wakefield) and Morley were ordered to muster with weapons. A £267 6s and 8d war tax was levied on Wakefield. **STANLEY** and **ALVERTHORPE** paid £109 14s and 4d.

SPEAK, HAROLD

A local Wakefield lad who left school at the age of fourteen to become a baker's boy selling bread from a bicycle basket, Speak pulled himself up by his bike clips and studied hard for a teaching qualification, securing the post of headmaster at the Cathedral School in 1959. He nurtured his school in its development, becoming one of the most respected members of his profession in the county. Speak was a gifted local historian and encouraged excavations at **SANDAL CASTLE** in 1963. He wrote a number of affectionate books about his native city including *Robin Hood of Wakefield, An Outline History of Wakefield* and *The Cathedral Church of All Saints Wakefield.*

SPINDLER, NELLIE

Dedicated and selfless Staff Nurse in Queen Alexandra's Imperial Military Nursing Service who, during World War I served in the 44th Casualty Clearing Station at Brandhoek on Belgium's Western Front. She became known as the 'Florence Nightingale of the North', attending a flood of casualties with great distinction particularly after the Battle of Passendale, the bombardment beginning on 31 July 1917. Her field hospital at Quaghebeurs Farm was located adjacent to a railway and a munitions dump and was frequently shelled. On 21 August 1917, incoming fire hit the wards and Spindler was critically injured, dying the same day. She was buried as the only woman alongside 10,779 soldiers in Lijssenthoek Cemetery near Ypres. Born in 1891, the daughter of a Wakefield police inspector, she was only twenty-six years old.

SPURN POINT COBBLES

Several thoroughfares in Wakefield were paved with cobbles dredged from the mouth of the Humber at Spurn Point and brought by barge to the city. Surviving cobbles can be seen in Barstow Square and in a yard behind the theatre.

STAGE COACHES

Wakefield was the terminus for the London coach during the seventeenth century. Passengers travelling to other destinations in the **WEST RIDING** would have to break their journeys in the town. The journey from London took four days in summer and up to eight days in winter. By 1785, four operators competed for passengers. The Leeds-Wakefield-Birmingham service was inaugurated in 1789, the Leeds-Wakefield-Bristol route opening in 1817. The first dedicated Leeds-Wakefield connection operated from 1809. Traffic dwindled dramatically with the coming of the railway in 1840 and four years later the era of the stagecoach was dead.

STAINTON, ELIZABETH DE

Prioress of Kirklees who infamously consorted with Sir Roger of Doncaster in conspiring the death of Robin **HOOD** by excessive bleeding. Her family came from **WOOLLEY**.

STANLEY

Ancient settlement at a strategic Roman fording point on the **CALDER RIVER**. Mining and canal haulage were the main occupations- it also had a jam factory - local entrepreneurs building three impressive mansions, **CLARKE HALL**, Stanley Hall and Hatfeild Hall. The village has a **BRASS BAND**.

STANLEY FERRY AQUEDUCT

This impressive listed structure – a Scheduled Ancient Monument which is unique in Europe - was designed by George Leather and opened for traffic on 9 August 1839, to carry Calder Cut barge traffic over the winding **CALDER RIVER**. It consists of two 155 feet long spanning bow-string girders weighing 110 tons each. These support a 940 ton trough of water 8 feet 6 inches deep. The design of the structure influenced that at Sydney Harbour in Australia.

STANLEY ROYD HOSPITAL

Former Victorian lunatic asylum and psychiatric hospital – the **WEST RIDING PAUPER LUNATIC ASYLUM**. Its site has recently been converted for office, leisure and residential use.

STANLEY, ST PETER'S CHURCH

Large and imposing edifice with distinctive twin battlemented towers built in 1824 using money voted by Parliament from the 'Million Fund' set up with reparation indemnities paid by the government of Austria following its involvement in the Napoleonic Wars. In one of the worst ever conflagrations in the district, the church was consumed by fire on 18th February 1911. The blaze started in a stove and soon took hold. The fire brigade were hampered in their attempts at dousing the flames as thirty brave members of the village institute entered the building and rescued its treasures. One valiant miner risked falling timbers and rang the belfry bell until he was knocked unconscious as he escaped. The tragedy gutted the whole interior of the church and destroyed the organ although the stone wall and the western end of the building were saved. The church was successfully rebuilt and re-opened in 1913. In the churchyard at the north-eastern corner of the church is the grave of the father of William H **BARTHOLOMEW**.

STAR INN

Ancient hostelry in Market Place, **PONTEFRACT**. In a description penned by a military man who, with two friends, visited Yorkshire in 1634, it is referred to as follows: 'We lighted at the Star, and took a fair repast to enable us to better scale that high and stately, famous and princely, impregnable castle and citadel, built by a Norman upon a rock, which for the situation, strength and largeness may be compared with any in this kingdom.' This important inn issued its own **TRADE TOKENS**.

STOLEN LOOT

At the time of the Reformation – the religious movement aimed at reforming abuses in the Catholic Church - zealots condemned the existence of images and statuary, iconoclasts breaking into churches to mutilate and steal. **WAKEFIELD CATHEDRAL** lost many of its treasures in the attacks but in 1756, a surprised householder in Northgate found twenty-five religious figures in his loft. These were assumed to have been plundered from the Wakefield church. According to contemporary reports, the discoveries were destroyed.

STONE HEAPS

This utilitarian sounding building at **WALTON** is believed to be the only surviving eighteenth century accommodation built specifically for navvies.

STOREY, DAVID

Wakefield born in 1933, this multiple award winning author, playwright and poet studied at **WAKEFIELD QUEEN ELIZABETH'S GRAMMAR SCHOOL** and the Slade School of Fine Art in London. He is a Fellow of University College, London. His landmark first novel *This Sporting Life* was published in 1960. It won the Macmillan Fiction Award and was adapted for a film starring Richard Harris who played a rugby player. Part of the film was shot in Wakefield on location at the Belle Vue rugby ground and elsewhere. During his stay in the city, Richard Harris stayed at the *Fox and Grapes* public house in Stanley Road. Subsequent novels include *Flight into Camden, Radcliffe, Saville, A Serious Man* and, most recently, (2004) *Thin-Ice Skater*. Storey's plays include *The Changing Room* and *The Farm*.

STRIKE

There have, of course, been industrial disputes in other industries in the district over the years but the mass withdrawal of pit labour during local and national strikes has had the most impact. There were miners' strikes in 1926, 1937, 1969, 1972, 1974 and 1984. The 1969 unofficial confrontation won a landmark eight hour day for surface workers and ushered in a new era of militancy in the industry following devastating pit closures in the 1950s and 1960s. In January 1972, the union called the first national strike since 1926. The conflict lasted seven weeks, firebrand unionist Arthur **SCARGILL** orchestrating mass picketing at the flashpoint 'Battle of Saltley Gates' in Birmingham. He was arrested twice during the dispute that forced the Conservative Government of Edward Heath to declare a state of emergency and to introduce a three-day week. In February 1974, a four weeks withdrawal of labour precipitated a General Election, the newly elected Labour administration treating with the miners and brokering long term improvements. By this time, wages were the highest amongst the British working class. The death knell of the industry was sounded in March 1984 when 187,000 miners embarked on a year-long strike - the longest running British industrial dispute of the twentieth century. At the time there were some 190,000 employees in the industry representing 170 pits. By this time, Arthur Scargill was the President of the National Union of Mineworkers and he was in the forefront of the battle with Margaret Thatcher. During the increasingly bitter and entrenched conflict, 11,000 people were arrested, 5,000 miners subsequently standing trial for a variety of offences. The dispute is estimated to have cost £3 billion. Throughout the ordeal, local women were prominent in carrying the fight and alleviating the suffering of miners' families, many being active in WAPC (Women Against Pit Closures). Men who broke ranks suffered the opprobrium of their neighbours, for them, the word 'blackleg' becoming one of the most venomously abusive words in the English language. On 8 April 1984, soup kitchens were provided for the first time in the industry since the 1920s and on the 17th of the month, Wakefield Council provided miners' schoolchildren with free meals during the Easter Holidays. The death of picket Joe **GREEN** galvanised every man. The strike ended with a return to work – many men proudly marched back with colliery brass bands playing – on 5th March 1985. Subsequent legislative strictures on the power of trade unions, particularly those outlawing secondary picketing, robbed the movement of its strength and an unstoppable round of pit closures followed. There are currently only 5000 workers in the industry operating from just twenty pits. Some forecasts predict the closure of these final twenty within a decade. After World War Two, the strike had the biggest impact on the district in the latter half of the twentieth century.

SUNNY LAWNS
One of the first residential homes for blind people set up in Wakefield under the provisions of the Blind Persons Act. The home was established in Carlton House, Sandy Walk, a property generously donated by Miss Elizabeth Childs – a cousin of Samuel Canning **CHILDS** – in 1924. It was used as a home for up to 20 blind men and women until 1968.

SUTCLIFFE, RICHARD
Pioneering Wakefield mining engineer and inventor of the underground coalface belt conveyor in 1905. His conveyor, which was introduced into coalmines in 1906, was provided with spring-loaded mangle pressure pulleys to eliminate belt slippage occurring with overloads. In 1949, his grandson Desmond initiated a study of friction on drive pulleys by fitting strain gauges, his investigations leading to further improvements in conveyor belt design.

SWAN INN, FERRYBRIDGE
At one time, this famous old coaching inn was reckoned to be second to none, none other that Sir Walter Scott sampling its hospitality and commenting: 'In 1737 and since, the best inn upon the great northern road.'

T

TAIT, DOCTOR ROBERT LAWSON
Brilliant pioneering surgeon known as the 'Father of Gynaecological Surgery'

who between 1867 and 1870 lived at Westgate End House in Wakefield, a residence long associated with the medical profession. Tait married Sybil Anne Stewart, the daughter of a Wakefield solicitor in the cathedral in 1871. In an era when animals were used routinely for medical experimentation, he attracted the opprobrium of some of his colleagues by calling for a total abandonment of vivisection. As a fledgling doctor of only twenty-one, he performed one of the first advanced ovariotomy operations – the removal of a tumour from an ovary - on 29th July 1868. He developed 'Tait's Operation' for chronic ovaritis, is credited with the first successful management of ectopic pregnancy, the first gall bladder and appendectomy operations and the development of pioneering techniques such as the removal of diseased Fallopian tubes. A keen anatomist, he set up a dissecting room at his surgery located above his coach house and stables. One clandestine visitor to the chamber recalled: 'In my early childhood days, there was still part of a dissected body, namely a scapula, arm and forearm and a hand, lying on the dissecting table. My brother and I used to get great kicks from this when we invited our school friends very secretly to inspect the exhibit.' Tait took up an appointment as surgeon at the Birmingham and Midlands Hospital for Women in 1871.He was an outspoken antivivisectionist, preferring investigative autopsy to experiments on animals. He wrote: '...the records teem with instances in which not only have animals fruitlessly been sacrificed, but human lives have been added to the list of victims by reason of its false light.' Speaking of his success in treating ovarian tumours to the Birmingham Philosophical Society – of the 139 ovariotomies he had performed by 1886, not one had resulted in death – he said: 'I have had, as is well known, some share in this advance and I say without hesitation that I have been led astray again and again by the published results of experiments on animals and I have to discard them entirely.'

TANSHELF

Suburb of **PONTEFRACT**, originally an Anglo-Saxon settlement. Over 100 skeletons were unearthed near the site of the Saxon church on The Booths.

TERRY, THOMAS:

Apprentice **FLANSHAW** handloom weaver with the dubious honour of being the first man hanged in York without a hood over his head. At his execution on 14 March 1803, he pulled off the blindfold and screamed his innocence, claiming that his accomplice Richard Heald had alone killed helpless widow Mrs E Smith. It took five men to get the noose over his head and he died protesting. Widow Smith was bludgeoned to death with a pair of tongs, her gravestone in the grounds of **WAKEFIELD WESTGATE CHAPEL** bearing an image of the murder weapon.

TEW, THOMAS WILLIAM

A distinguished member of a banking family, Tew successfully developed his **PONTEFRACT** and Wakefield based business, opening branches in **NORMANTON, CASTLEFORD, ACKWORTH, FEATHERSTONE, HEMSWORTH** and **SOUTH ELMSALL**. He was a noted historian, philanthropist and freemason. His bank was one of the last in the country to issue its own banknotes. Examples of these may be seen in **PONTEFRACT MUSEUM**. The bank was absorbed by Barclays in 1906. Tew renovated and improved **CARLETON GRANGE** in the 1880's.

THOMPSON, BEN

In the Wild West hall of fame, his notches are up there with those of Wild Bill Hickcock and Wyatt Earp. This prolific gunslinger from **KNOTTINGLEY** was the son of a mariner. He was born in a house on Aire Street, St Botolph's Church recording his baptism in 1842. After attending local schools, in 1851 at the age nine, he moved with his family to Texas, where in 1860, as an eighteen year old, he was part of a posse on the heels of a party of Indian kidnappers. He shot and killed the leader of the band and heroically rescued a group of children. Afterwards, he joined and quit the Confederate Army, fought with the French in the Mexican conflict and returned to Texas, becoming the proprietor of a number of gambling saloons. He killed another man in a shoot-out, spending some time in the State Penitentiary. On his release, he bought the *Bulls Head Saloon* in Abilene in Kansas and then another in Fort Elliot Texas where he met the legendary Bat Masterson, the bullet-flying encounter inspiring a whole genre of cowboy films. Masterson had been shot in the leg by an assailant who he had killed in a gunfight. Other desperadoes were about to finish him off when Thompson coolly intervened, flourishing a Colt in each hand and saying: 'Move and you're dead men. Put up your hands and get out.' After the incident, Thompson and Masterson became best friends. Thompson later hit the bottle and developed a fearsome reputation for shooting-up the town. One of his party pieces was to shoot off the hats of salesmen as they unsuspectingly strode down the main street. And, in defining- Hollywood style, he would rake saloons with gunfire and blast down chandeliers. He gunned down two more men in acknowledged self- defence and then in 1881, decided to run for election as Austin's Chief of Police! He was elected and gave up drinking. After another death – his attacker made the fatal mistake of giving away his position by peeping through the slats of a Venetian blind – Thompson resigned his position and died from a hail of eight bullets in a San Antonio theatre in 1884. He was forty-three. With a lightning draw and a fearsome reputation, he had gunned down 16 men. 'It is doubtful if, in his lifetime, there was another man living to equal him in the speed of draw with a gun. He was absolutely without fear and his nerves were those of the finest steel.' So said the Sheriff of Dodge City, Bat Masterson. Ben's brother Bill was also a noted gunman.

THORNES HOUSE
Brick mansion erected for James **MILNES** to designs by John **CARR** between 1779 and 1781. The luxuriously appointed property, which had an ironwork and glass hothouse, was fitted out by Josiah Wedgwood, its later treasures including Sevres porcelain collected by the owner in 1792.

THORPE AUDLIN
Former agricultural settlement that during the Middle Ages was an important source of limestone.

TOE SUCKER
In an age of eccentrics Charles **WATERTON** stuck out like a sore thumb. An oddball of the first water, a man who nightly slept on a wooden pillow and indulged in daily rituals of blood letting, he was unconventional in the extreme. Driven by an abiding fascination for wild animals, he visited South America where he rode on the back of a cayman, gagging the animal with his own braces. He also collected curare for later experimentation and studied the behaviour of bats. Being a dedicated user of the blood-letting razor and what he termed his 'claret bowl' he had a natural affection for the blood-sucking propensities of the vampire bat so he was determined to experience their pricks at first hand. So he exposed a toe, sleeping with this single appendage protruding from his bunk as a bat was allowed free flit of his bedroom. Weeks passed without a single nip. The shunned Waterton was upset and complained bitterly noting that his Indian servant had all the fun. This poor chap was perforated nightly and became so anaemic that he could hardly stand. 'His toe,' explained Waterton, 'held all the attractions.' Closer to home in 1834, the squire had an unlikely encounter with a nest of deadly rattlesnakes in Leeds. Twenty-eight of the reptiles had been collected in order to test, before a body of eminent doctors, the anti-venom properties of Waterton's curare – a native concoction he had collected in South America. A problem arose. How would the snakes be transferred from their box to the unfortunate victims? The dare-devil intervened and coolly grabbed a beast by the neck. The rattlesnake was induced to bite a guinea pig and was soon returned to its box. The procedure was repeated. Then, abruptly, one of the reptiles made a dart for freedom, just as Waterton had his hand half way out of the box. All the learned doctors rushed into the street in blind panic without their hats but the squire gingerly removed his hand, slammed the lid shut and returned the escapee in one fearless flourish.

TOLFREE, SYDNEY

Early cinema proprietor who came to Yorkshire in 1906 as the manager of the **WAKEFIELD HIPPODROME** where he organised performances screened from a bioscope. He formed the Wakefield Picture House Company and built his 1460 seat Picture House – the town's first purpose built cinema – on Upper Westgate in 1913, opening the show with *The Last Days of Pompeii*. The theatre, which had a versatile interior design to accommodate concerts and dramas, was renamed The Playhouse and refurbished in 1921 when an organ was installed. Tolfree left that year to manage the Futurist cinema in Scarborough.

TOM PUDDINGS

Coal-carrying compartment boats or barges used extensively on the **AIRE AND CALDER NAVIGATION**. Multiply-towed in series by tugs, they were first introduced by William H **BARTHOLOMEW** in the 1860's. The boats had a carrying capacity of 40 tons, their number reaching an all-time high of 1010 in 1913 when they carried a record-breaking tonnage of coal and general cargo to Goole of 2,860,315 tons. The leading boat, when loaded, was fitted with a false bow called a Jebus to prevent handling impairment by bow waves.

Tom Puddings at Ferrybridge. LMA

TRADE TOKENS

The earliest coinage in general circulation in England from the Norman Conquest to the reign of Queen Elizabeth I, was minted in silver and gold. Many of the coins, particularly in silver, were miniscule in size and weight (the Elizabethan halfpenny weighed only four grains) and were lost in circulation soon after issue. This prompted the need for a local remedy to replace the lack of small change and up to twenty thousand different varieties of token were produced locally in England, Wales and Ireland until the practice was outlawed by a proclamation of the king. Both Wakefield and **PONTEFRACT** produced tokens. One of the most interesting of the Wakefield tokens was struck by John Naylor, who was probably a son of James **NAYLOR**. It is stamped on the obverse IOHH. NAYLOR. GROCER and shows a soldier on horseback with his sword drawn. It is dated 1664. Equally as fascinating is a 1666 **PONTEFRACT** token issued by the **STAR INN** in Market Place. It is marked **YE STAR** and shows a blazing star on the obverse. Both tokens are now prized collectors items.

TRAFFIC LIGHTS

The first set of automatic traffic lights in Wakefield dispensed with the services of one point-duty policeman. They were erected at the junction of Ings Road and Denby Dale Road in 1929. Signals at the junction of Northgate and Howard Street were installed a few years later.

TREACY, ERIC

Born in London of Irish parents in 1907, he was Bishop of Wakefield from 1968 to 1976. A steam railway enthusiast from 1936 when he was inducted into his first living in Liverpool, he rose through the ecclesiastical ranks to become Bishop Suffragan and Archdeacon of **PONTEFRACT** in 1961. An orator of great wit, lucidity and charm, he was a self-confessed baiter of Yorkshiremen but they loved him for it. He had particular fondness for miners. Commenting on the **LOFTHOUSE PIT DISASTER** in 1973 he said: 'The mining industry is a world of dust and danger to which so many people have been condemned so that the country might have prosperity.' The bishop regularly visited the inmates of **WAKEFIELD PRISON** where he was presented with a portrait of himself, which became a prized possession. He died in 1978 while photographing the steam engine *Evening Star* at Appleby Station. 'A man of granite with the heart of a child', he will forever be remembered as 'Wakefield's Railway Bishop.' He donated a bishop's throne to the cathedral in 1974. The Bishop Treacy Memorial Hall adjacent to the cathedral was opened in 1982. One of his most memorable sayings is this: 'Yorkshiremen are suspicious, obstinate, nonconformist and blunt...and I like them as they are.'

TURNPIKE ROAD

The first Turnpike Act was passed in 1663. It empowered JP's to levy tolls on road users and to use the revenue for the repair and maintenance of highways. Operators were required to build toll-houses like the remaining structure at **WRAGBY BAR** and to install turnpike gates at strategic points in the road. The new roads were largely promoted by wealthy landowners, driven by commercial interests or the need to improve access to their estates. These turnpikes were, at first, very unpopular with the public. Local feeling was hostile to the imposition of charges and there was a great deal of bribery of gate-keepers. Riots ensued, lawless bands pulling down gates and setting fire to toll houses. Eventually, this original idea for the modern concept of road pricing spread throughout the country, contributing greatly to economic prosperity. One of the district's most notable turnpike roads was built from Aberford to Wakefield using virgin land and part of the line of the **GREAT NORTH ROAD** described as 'very crooked and indirect...and so narrow as not to admit carts and other carriages in many parts.' It was authorised under a Parliamentary Act of 1789 and was perhaps the first road to be built in the county using modern constructional techniques. Toll bars were erected at Stanley Green, Swillington Bridge and Garforth Moor. In October 1869 an irate resident wrote to the *Pontefract Advertiser* complaining that a tollbooth had been illegally set up at the Mill Hill Gate in East Hardwick. Money had, he claimed, been collected without the necessary authority since 1856. 'The lawless highwayman demands your money or your life,' he argued. 'The unlawful gatekeeper claims your money, or forbids you to pass. Where's the difference?'

U

UPTON

Former mining village in an area once dominated by King Coal. Its colliery site has been transformed in recent years into a limestone heath covered in flowers, a former local railway line being integrated into the route of a country walk. A memorial remembers the miners who lost their lives at Upton Colliery between 1926 and 1964, the legacy of mining infusing the work of local celebrity John **GODBER**.

UPTON BEACON

At 300 metres above sea level with views of York Minster, the Lincolnshire Wolds and the hills of Derbyshire the site was ideal for use as a beacon station in an early-warning chain that would have announced the approach of the Armada. The beacon has been replaced by a prominent water tower.

V

VIBRATION WHITE FINGER

Also referred to as 'Dead Man's Fingers', a form of Reyaud's Disease caused by a lack of blood flow to the hands and feet, the extremities becoming white, numb and painful. Although more prevalent among women, it is a common ailment of miners, who use vibrating chain saws and drills. An afflicted miner brought a test case to court in 1997, and in a landmark decision, British Coal were ordered to pay compensation. The Government appealed, but the ruling was upheld, a subsequent out-of-court settlement sanctioning the biggest compensation deal in history. The ruling will eventually benefit up to 140,000 British miners who will receive some £2 billion.

VICAR OF WAKEFIELD

The immortal book *The Vicar of Wakefield* by Oliver Goldsmith may well have been inspired by Benjamin Wilson who was vicar of **NORMANTON** in 1727 and of Wakefield in 1751. He died in Wakefield in 1764.

VIVIAN, MONA

This pantomime star was probably born around 1895. A miner's daughter who lived in a cottage on Ings Road, she was a child prodigy, appearing at her local **WAKEFIELD HIPPODROME** theatre by the age of four. A year later, she was known as 'Wee Mona'. The family moved to Rhyl in Wales where Vivian became a principal pantomime girl and boy. She shot to fame between 1910 and 1920 and starred in shows in Bradford, Sheffield, Leeds and London. With a good singing voice, she briefly recorded for Columbia and her portrait appeared on the front cover of the *Sunday Chronicle's Pantomime Annual*. One of her fervent admirers bubbled: 'Don't say sparkling champagne...say Mona Vivian!' The lady was indeed attractive and married the millionaire chairman of Leeds United Football Club.

VOYSEY, CHARLES

Renowned British architect and interior designer responsible for the design of the attractive grade two listed *Rising Sun Inn* in Whitwood, **CASTLEFORD**. The inn was built in 1908 as the Institute of Briggs Colliery. It marries well with Voysey's well-ordered terrace of nearby cottages. Voysey was the first British domestic architect to gain an international reputation. He also designed textiles, furniture and wallpapers.

W

WAKEFIELD
County town of the old **WEST RIDING** occupying an eminence above the **CALDER RIVER**. A Saxon settlement in the tenth century centred on three roads – Northgate, Westgate and Kirkgate - which ran down to the Roman ford on the river, the town flourished around its church of All Hallows and became a busy agricultural centre. It developed important cloth weaving and hosiery industries (nearly 2,600 people were employed in 1911) other local products including iron and coal coming to dominate the regional economy in the nineteenth century and in the early part of the twentieth century. Wakefield became a Metropolitan District in 1974 after Local Government Reorganisation, the new District Council absorbing thirteen former administrative authorities. There are Wakefield's in Jamaica, Kansas, Michigan, Nebraska, New Zealand, Quebec, Rhode Island and Virginia. The city has its own metropolitan **BRASS BAND**.

WAKEFIELD 41
Industrial estate straddling the A650 portal into the city with immediate access to Junction 41 of the M1.

WAKEFIELD ART GALLERY
Displaying mainly twentieth century drawings and paintings, many of local interest, the gallery houses impressive collections of works by Barbara **HEPWORTH**, Henry **MOORE** and Roland **PITCHFORK**. It has a pleasant and relaxing sculpture garden.

WAKEFIELD'S BLACK WHITSUNDAY
During the Civil War, Wakefield was a Royalist stronghold, held, on 20 May 1643, by three thousand foot under the command of Sir Francis Mackworth and seven troops of horse led by General Goring. While Goring and his officers were carousing at **HEATH HALL** – they spent the afternoon playing bowls after a night of heavy drinking – a numerically inferior Roundhead force was planning an attack on the town. They struck without warning in the early hours of Whitsunday, overwhelming two troops of men stationed at **STANLEY** and proceeding to Wakefield at about four o'clock in the morning. Driving musketeers from the hedges, they assaulted 'Wrengate and Northgate; and after an hour and a half fight, recovered one of their peeces, and turned it upon them, and entered the town at both places, at one and the same time.' Goring, Sir Thomas Bland, other officers of note and fifteen hundred soldiers were taken prisoner, the number of men captured

exceeding that of the attacking force. On the following Saturday, a jubilant Parliament resolved: 'That a public thanksgiving should be given, in all the churches and chapels of London etc for the good success it had pleased God to give the forces under the command of the Lord Fairfax, at the taking in of Wakefield.'

WAKEFIELD BREAD STREET
Formerly Ratten Row and, earlier still, Breadbooths, taking its name from the bakers who once traded there.

WAKEFIELD CATHEDRAL
Dating from the fourteenth and fifteenth centuries, this magnificent skyline building in the centre of the city became a cathedral in 1888. At 247 feet, it has the highest spire in Yorkshire. Its treasures include a font of 1661, a rood screen of 1635, several whimsical misericords and a collection of fine stained glass.

WAKEFIELD CATTLE MARKET
In its heyday, the market was the largest in the north of England, processing some half a million animals in the 1870s and 1880s. It was bought by Wakefield Council in 1938 and finally closed in 1965.

WAKEFIELD CIVIC SOCIETY
Formed in 1964 with the intention of preserving the buildings, environment and historical heritage of Wakefield. The society has a prestigious design awards scheme and is responsible for erecting blue information plaques on significant city buildings. It jointly sponsored the creation of the **GISSINGS CENTRE** and has contributed to civic renewal schemes such as the reinstatement of Wakefield's characteristic narrow yards.

Wakefield Cathedral spire, the tallest in Yorkshire. LMA

WAKEFIELD CLARENCE PARK

Extensive public park provided from funds largely donated by local businessmen and dignitaries and opened in a grand civic ceremony attended by thousands of jubilant citizens on 6th July 1893. The first of Wakefield's public parks was accessed by nearly two miles of brightly planted footpaths and avenues, a double row of one hundred and eight horse chestnuts providing a leafy honour guard alongside a spectacular carriage drive. The inaugural festivities were accompanied by the ringing of the cathedral bells and the release of fire balloons.

WAKEFIELD COLLEGE

The principal further education establishment in the district operating from several sites. The college has developed flexible learning programmes in all subject areas providing for basic skills training to the highest level of professional and vocational qualifications.

Wakefield College. LMA

WAKEFIELD COUNTY HALL

Another prominent city-centre skyline building erected between 1894 and 1898 as the **WEST RIDING** County Offices. Architect's Gibson and Russell's winning competition entry incorporates an eye-catching polygonal corner tower surmounted by a dome, dormer gables and oriel windows. Internally, the building is sumptuously furnished with tropical hardwoods, marble and a collection of exquisite sculptures and friezes, one frieze in the ante room to the council chamber showing scenes from the **WARS OF THE ROSES**, including the Battle of **WAKEFIELD GREEN**.

WAKEFIELD CRIB

Unique and beautiful nativity scene sculpted for **WAKEFIELD CATHEDRAL** by Austin Wright in 1955. The woven backcloth is by Theo Moorman. The work, which is on permanent display to the left of the altar, was restored in 1999.

Wakefield County Hall. LMA

Wakefield County Hall. LMA

WAKEFIELD CROWN COURT HOUSE

Part of the imperial collection of buildings in the heart of the city, this impressive structure built in 1810 has a tetrastyle Greek Doric portico and pediment. It was completed in 1810. Before that date, magistrates had to administer the law from local public houses. The building was extended in 1848 and again in the 1880s but it was controversially closed in 1973.

WAKEFIELD CROSS

Originally dating from around AD 940 and erected in the cathedral yard, the cross was mutilated at the time of the Reformation and was discovered acting as a makeshift doorstep in a shop in 1862. It was removed to York in 1870 and now resides in St Mary's Abbey in the city. Wakefield has a 1933 replica – base to crosspiece – to the right of the cathedral altar.

WAKEFIELD DRURY LANE LIBRARY

Opened in 1906, the library was provided mainly through the generosity of Scot Andrew Carnegie, the multi-millionaire who made a fortune in America developing railroads. He gave £8000 to the project and devoted $12 million to endowing 660 libraries in the UK. Bradford magistrate Charles Skidmore donated 2000 books to the library, mainly about Wakefield and its district. Carnegie was present at the unveiling ceremony. With unabashed brass neck, the mayor told the benefactor: 'All things considered, a good Scotsman was not much inferior to a Yorkshireman.' The design of the library was controversial. One detractor said: 'The whole edifice conveys the impression of a somewhat extravagant nobleman's stable, an ambitious municipal abattoir or a rather stylish auction mart.'

WAKEFIELD ELIZABETHAN GRAMMAR SCHOOL

Established in 'a retired and silent quarter of the town' in 1598, the school in what is now Brook Street, became the Green Coat School, transferred from premises in Westgate in the 1850's. One of that school's original masters – John Bradford – was appointed on the understanding that: 'He will not play at cards or dice or any other unlawful game during the said term. Alehouses or Taverns of Custom he will not haunt nor contract matrimony nor commit adultery with any woman during the said term. Latterly, the school became attached to **WAKEFIELD CATHEDRAL**, teaching choirboys 'to chant and sing anthems'. In recent years, the building has been restored and used as an exhibition and meeting centre.

WAKEFIELD-EMLEY AFC

Amalgamated Unibond Premier Division soccer club known as the Pewits. They play at Belle Vue in Wakefield. In 1988, **EMLEY** reached the Final of the FA Vase at Wembley. In 1998, the club played West Ham in the FA Cup, only loosing 2-1 before a crowd of nearly 18,000 at Upton Park.

WAKEFIELD EMPIRE THEATRE
A beautifully appointed theatre designed by Frank Matcham and opened in 1909 in Kirkgate. The theatre had its own orchestra.

WAKEFIELD EUROPORT
 Inter-modal, fully serviced 350 acres (142 ha) industrial development site – Yorkshire's largest - at Junction 31 of the M62 Motorway offering daily rail services to continental Europe via the Channel Tunnel.

WAKEFIELD EXPRESS
Local newspaper first published by gaslight on a steam-powered press in March 1852 by John Robinson in his Southgate premises, which are still in use today. The price of the first edition was 4¹/₂ old pence. The first edition of the *Pontefract and Castleford Express* was published in 1880. The *Hemsworth and South Elmsall Express* was born in 1912. In 2000, the *Wakefield Express* was named as Newspaper of the Year for Yorkshire and the North East.

WAKEFIELD FIRST
The Development Agency for the Wakefield District, established in partnership with the local authority, Yorkshire Forward, the Mid-Yorkshire Chamber of Commerce, **WAKEFIELD COLLEGE** and the local job centre to provide a single point of contact for business and investment enquiries.

WAKEFIELD GIRLS' HIGH SCHOOL
Fee paying private school established in 1878 as a scion of **WAKEFIELD QUEEN ELIZABETH'S GRAMMAR SCHOOL**, originally taking 59 pupils. Its motto is: 'EACH FOR ALL AND ALL FOR GOD'. Notable past pupils include Dame Barbara **HEPWORTH**, Helen **FIELDING** and Joanne **HARRIS**.

WAKEFIELD GREEN, BATTLE OF
Fought out in a snowstorm on the 30 December 1460, this bloody contest between the rival houses of York and Lancaster ended in defeat for the white rose. The Duke of York sallied from his garrison at **SANDAL CASTLE** and engaged the forces of Lord Clifford, the duke and 2000 of his men perishing in the action. Clifford, who was henceforth known as 'Bloody Clifford', intercepted the duke's seventeen year old son and killed him with a stab wound to the heart. The duke's head was afterwards cut off and placed on the

Depiction of the Battle of Wakefield Green in a frieze in Wakefield County Hall. LMA

parapet of Clifford's Tower in York 'So York may overlook the town of York.'
His body meanwhile was buried in the Cluniac Priory of St John in
PONTEFRACT. Prisoners were marched to London and incarcerated in a
dungeon renamed the **WAKEFIELD TOWER**. On 22 July 1466, King
Edward IV honoured his father with a splendid funeral at Fotheringay. The
duke's body was exhumed and reburied with great ceremony and memorial
crosses were erected in **SANDAL MAGNA** and Kirkgate, Wakefield. The
exact spot where the duke fell was long marked by three willow trees.
Although these were lost in a storm in 1866, they are still remembered in an
old local saying: 'Mind the Duke of York without his head doesn't git hod o'
thee as tha gans by the willow trees.' The citizens of Wakefield erected their
own tribute to the fallen knight on part of the Manygates School site:

'Richard Plantagenet, Duke of York, fighting for the cause of the White
Rose, fell on this spot in the Battle of Wakefield, December 30th 1460.

This stone is erected in 1897 by some who wish to preserve the traditional site.'

In 1461, at Towton near Tadcaster, Richard's death was avenged in a crushing defeat for the Lancastrians, the victor, Edward, becoming the first king - Edward IV- of the dynastic House of York.

WAKEFIELD HIPPODROME

Short-lived prefabricated entertainment palace opened in Teall Street, Wakefield in 1903. It was known as the 'Tin Tabernacle'. It was 162 feet long by 60 feet wide by 40 feet high. It offered all types of entertainment – circuses, equestrian events, music hall and short films. A number of celebrated acts appeared under its tin roof, the famous roll-call including Gracie Fields and Harry Houdini.

WAKEFIELD INDUSTRIAL AND FINE ARTS EXHIBITION

Prestigious and highly successful exposition of local arts and crafts hosted in Wakefield in 1865. Conceptually it began as a low-key parochial celebration of the achievements of local school children. The idea caught the spirit and imagination of the age and the project snowballed drawing interest from all over Yorkshire, inventors, manufacturers, industrialists, artisans and artists clamouring for space in a temporary exhibition hall erected on a site in Wood Street now occupied by **WAKEFIELD TOWN HALL**. Some displays were accommodated in **WAKEFIELD TAMMY HALL**. Enormous varieties of themed stands displayed chemical products, glassware, earthenware, ceramics, tools, ironmongery, metalwork, clothing, furniture, paintings, jewellery, fancy goods and models. The organisers awarded medals for the most outstanding entries. The exhibition, which was held from 30 August until 19 October, attracted 189,423 visitors and made a handsome profit of over £3000.

WAKEFIELD KIRKGATE RAILWAY STATION

The railway first came to the city in 1840 with termini in Leeds and Hebden Bridge. The course of the **CALDER RIVER** had to be diverted to access the town. The advent of the line was received with only muted enthusiasm and vested interests in the Aire and Calder Navigation Company, who feared they would loose business to their rival, rather churlishly objected to the design of the Kirkgate Bridge, taking the dispute, unsuccessfully, to a tribunal. The local press only made a brief reference to the new line although local people showed more interest, 'hundreds of people visiting the station house, Primrose Hill and other places to get sight of the trains.' The first station house cost £453 and was not much more than 'a small cottage in size.' It was replaced in 1854.

This time, the **WAKEFIELD EXPRESS** was more appreciative: 'When looked at in contrast with the diminutive building which must still be fresh in the recollection of the travelling public of Wakefield, and which could only be considered an excuse for a station, the present erections have certainly a very imposing appearance and every inhabitant must feel that besides being better calculated to meet the wants of passengers, are at the same time more in keeping with the principal corn and cattle markets in the North of England.'

WAKEFIELD MEDIA AND CREATIVITY CENTRE

Civic Quarter development offering exhibition, public meeting and office facilities for media enterprises. The centre will include the Art of Propaganda Gallery.

WAKEFIELD METROPOLITAN DISTRICT COUNCIL

Formed under local government reorganisation on 1 April 1974, the council, with its headquarters in Wakefield, absorbed thirteen former authorities. One of five metropolitan districts in West Yorkshire, it covers some 350 kilometres and embraces a population of 318, 000. The council employs over 15,000 people throughout the district.

WAKEFIELD MUSEUM

Situated on **WOOD STREET, WAKEFIELD**, the museum is housed in a Grecian styled building built as public rooms in 1820-21 and inscribed 'MECHANICS INSTITUTE' on the frieze. The public rooms had salons on the first floor and a suite of public baths, a public dispensary, a physician's surgery and an apothecary's shop in the basement. The building later became the Institute of Literature and Science. Its Waterton Room tells the stirring life story of adventurer and explorer Charles **WATERTON**, his pioneering taxidermy specimens forming eye-catching displays. The ancient and modern history of Wakefield is described in a series of tableaux that include 'Wakefield at War.' The museum has almost 100,000 items and an invaluable and fascinating collection of 10,000 historic photographs accessed through a touch-screen computer.

WAKEFIELD OPERA HOUSE

Elegant replacement theatre for impresario Benjamin **SHERWOOD**, designed by the leading specialist architect Frank Matcham and opened in Drury Lane in 1894. It cost £13,000. Gas-lit, it had a richly framed proscenium and Rococo plasterwork. It took some while for local citizens to enjoy its opulence and sophistication, one commentator lamenting: 'The majority of Wakefield people can only appreciate the rottenest of melodramas

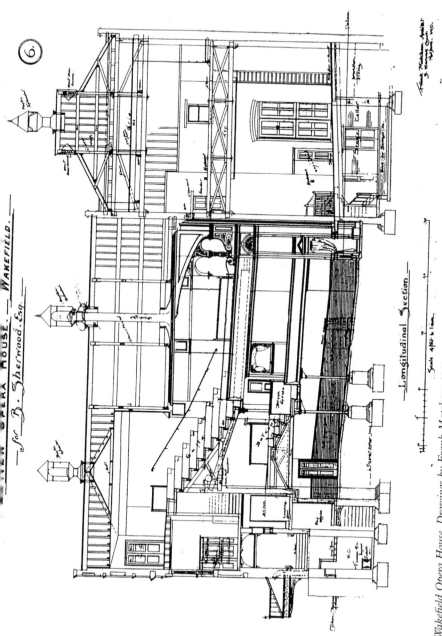

Wakefield Opera House. Drawings by Frank Matcham. LMA

Theatre, Wakefield.

On THURSDAY, October 27th, 1825,

Will be presented (for the first time)

A NEW MUSICAL PERFORMANCE

Of an Extraordinary Character, called

DER FREISCHUTZ;

Or, the Seventh Bullet!

(WITH THE ORIGINAL AND CELEBRATED OVERTURE.)

This eccentric vehicle for Music, is the Translation from that highly celebrated German Opera, composed by Carl Maria Weber.

The Music under the superintendence of Mr. Pindar; the Scenery by Messrs. Dearlove, W. Remington, and Assistants; the Machinery by Mr. Boyles; the Monsters and Properties by a London Artist and Mr. Yarnold; the Dresses by Mr. Smithers and Assistants.

Ottocar (a Bohemian Prince)	Mr WEBSTER
Bernhard, (Ranger of the Forest)	Mr FAULKNER
Adolph, (a Huntsman)	Mr BELLAMY
Caspar, (Ditto)	Mr CALLAGHAN
Rollo, (Ditto)	Mr WALTON
Killian, (a Villager)	Mr W. J. HAMMOND
Zamiel, (the Black Yager, or Huntsman Spirit of the Forest)	Mr MASON
Witch of the Glen	Mr W. REMINGTON
Demon of the Hartz . . . Mr. MILLS . Linda . Miss STAFFORD	

(Her Third Appearance.)

Rose . . Mrs. CALLAGHAN . Bridesmaid . . Miss H. LACY

Foresters—Messrs Andrews, Stanley, Thompson, Johnson, &c.

Peasants—Mesdames Andrews, French, Webster, W. J. Hammond, &c.

A GERMAN WALTZ,

By MISS H. LACY, MESDAMES CALLAGHAN, W. J. HAMMOND, and ANDREWS.

The Scenes, Incidents, and Characteristic Pieces of Music occur in the following order:

ACT I.

SCENE I.—Outskirts of Forest and Village Inn.—The National Trial of Skill in Shooting at a Target.—Grand Chorus of Peasants and Yagers, or Huntsmen.—March and Procession of Villagers, &c.—SONG, Killian, and Laughing Chorus.—National Waltz.—BUCCHANALIAN SONG, Caspar.—The appearance of ZAMIEL.—The effects of a Magic Bullet.—BRAVURA, Adolph.

ACT II.

SCENE I.—Room in the Ranger's House.

SCENE 2.—The WOLF's GLEN.—Full Moon, shining dimly.—A Cataract.—Chorus of Invisible Spirits, as the Clock strikes Twelve.—Grand and Impressive Music, preparatory to the Incantation.

THEATRE ROYAL, WAKEFIELD.

LICENSED ACCORDING TO ACT OF PARLIAMENT.

Lessees:—Messrs. Robinson and Crofton.

NEW STAGE, NEW SCENERY, REFITTED WITH GAS,

AND THE INTERIOR BEAUTIFULLY RE-DECORATED.

A New Act Drop the Church of Santa Maria della Salute, Venice,

PAINTED BY MR. GEORGE MARTIN.

On Tuesday, September 16th, 1851,

The Performance will commence with

BERTRAM

Or, the Castle of St. Aldobrand.

PAS DE OLIO, BY MISS JULIET POWER.

After which,

LOAN OF A LOVER!

An Irish Lilt, by Miss SALMON.

The whole to conclude with the Laughable Farce of

THE ETON BOY !!

Acting Manager ... Mr. CRofton. Stage Manager ... Mr. REYNOLDS. Prompter ... Mr. WALTON.

Scene Painter ... Mr. GEO. MARTIN. Properties ... Mr. FIELDING. Leader of the Orchestra ... Mr. DEWHIRST.

Prices of Admission.

DRESS BOXES, 2s. 6d. SIDE BOXES, 1s. 6d. PIT, 1s. GAL. 6d.

Doors Open at Seven o'Clock Performance to commence at half-past precisely.

ROBINSON AND CROFTON, PRINTERS, SILVER STREET, WAKEFIELD.

Wakefield Opera House posters. LMA

---

or the vulgarist of leg shows.' In 1901, the *Wakefield Herald* commented: 'The average Wakefield theatre-goer is happy so long as you give him a liberal sprinkling of violence and a few strong situations.'

WAKEFIELD PARK HILL GARDENS

Open horticultural parkland on the east of the city given over, at the beginning of the 19th century, to strawberry gardens and extensive orchards. 'One of our real pleasures on Saturday afternoons', recalls local historian Henry **CLARKSON** in his book *Memories of Merry Wakefield*, 'was to go to Park Hill Gardens and enjoy the delicious strawberries and cream to be had for a very modest sum. The strawberries were always fine, the sunny slope of the hill suiting them well.' The fruit was displaced in turn by the cement works of Joseph **ASPDIN** and **WAKEFIELD KIRKGATE RAILWAY STATION**.

WAKEFIELD PRISON

The prison was originally built as a house of correction in 1595 on a site near Back Lane and Westgate. It was funded from a £20 legacy in the will of George **SAVILE** who lived at nearby Haselden Hall in Northgate. Additional works were carried out in 1611. At that time, men and women were incarcerated together and were restrained with leg irons in filthy conditions. Following an escape in 1764, the authorities commissioned the eminent architect John **CARR** to design a new facility. In 1880 further extensions were added and then in 1847, a much enlarged and improved 732-cell prison was opened. A wonder of the age, it was the largest and best equipped of its kind in the world. Each cell was fitted with a hammock, a small round table, a three-legged stool and gas lighting and the inmates were allowed to wash in warm water every two weeks. Other accoutrements included a slop house and a treadmill. The prison was noted for its experiments in prison reform. In much the same way as public schools, the inmates were allocated to different 'houses' each house leader or 'stroke' wearing a distinctive tie. Competition was encouraged, privileges were bestowed and prisoners were allowed to earn money. The current prison is largely based on the 1847 footprint. In 1966, the prison was designated as a dispersal unit and, chillingly, as ' a life centre with a focus on serious sex offenders.' It has a modern capacity of 581.

WAKEFIELD QUEEN ELIZABETH'S GRAMMAR SCHOOL

Founded at the request of the leading citizens of Wakefield, this fee-paying school received its royal charter from Queen Elizabeth I in 1591. In 1854, it moved to its present site in Northgate, into premises formerly occupied by the West Riding Preparatory School erected in 1833 and 1834. The building has an imposing Gothic façade in honey-coloured stone. Notable past pupils include Edmund **CARTWRIGHT**, Kenneth **LEIGHTON**, John George

Wakefield Queen Elizabeth's Grammar School. LMA

HAIGH, David **STOREY**, Lord **WOLFENDEN**, Reginald Moxon **ARMITAGE**, Roland Vivian **PITCHFORK**, Phillip **MICKMAN** and Michael **HARRISON**. One of the school's notable maths masters was John Alfred Disraeli **BEAVEN**. In 1878, the school integrated with **WAKEFIELD GIRLS' HIGH SCHOOL**. The joint schools advertise themselves as 'The friendliest schools in Yorkshire and the North!'

WAKEFIELD RACECOURSE

A document survives stipulating the rules governing the first horse races to be held on 'Wakefield Ings' on Monday 1 and Wednesday 3 September 1740. Jockeys would compete for a purse of £50 and two silver plates over a course of three miles. Race entrants were to make application in Wakefield's *Black Swan*. Every 'horse, mate or gelding which shall be so entered the sum of ten shillings and sixpence and two shillings for every one weighed.' In 1745, racing was transferred from the Ings to **OUTWOOD**. The last meeting was held there in 1794.

WAKEFIELD SOUTH PARADE

Elegant terrace of Georgian houses with Tuscan and Ionic doorways. This quiet oasis close to the city centre still has its private gardens.

WAKEFIELD ST JOHN'S NORTH

Elegant Georgian terraced development a few hundred yards north-east of the town centre, centrally pedimented with Tuscan porches.

WAKEFIELD ST JOHN'S SQUARE

Intended quadrangle of Georgian terraced housing (the fourth side was never built) embracing the beautiful late eighteenth century church of St John's.

WAKEFIELD TAMMY HALL

Built in 1778 for the display and sale of tammies – specialist types of worsted cloths manufactured in the mid-Calder and Upper Dearne valleys – the hall was a two storey construction, each floor measuring 70 yards by 10 yards, the sales area accommodating display stands for

Wakefield St John's Square. LMA

around 200 manufacturers. To signal the opening of each days trading, the hall-keeper would ring a bell housed above the hall in an elegant cupola. The vacant hall was used as display space for **WAKEFIELD INDUSTRIAL AND FINE ARTS EXHIBITION** in 1865. Part of the building was demolished to provide space for the erection of **WAKEFIELD TOWN HALL** and the remaining structure was converted for use as a police and fire station between 1877 and 1879.

WAKEFIELD THORNHILL STREET SCHOOL
Elegantly symmetrical school with quoins and a classical central pediment, opened in 1846 for the children of Methodists. It became the Urban Studies Centre.

WAKEFIELD TOWER
Regarded as 'the strongest fortress in the land' this fortification in the Tower of London was the obvious repository for the Crown Jewels. Together with the Royal Regalia, they were transferred here in 1870 although they now reside in a new exhibition centre close by. The tower was built at the time of Henry II. Its name probably derives from that of William de Wakefield, a king's clerk who was appointed in 1344. In 1346, Wakefield became the vicar of St Helen's Church in **SANDAL MAGNA**. It would seem that he left his post as Keeper of the Changes in the Tower under a cloud, the king ordering that the goods he had brought with him to Yorkshire be seized and sold to swell the sovereign's purse.

Wakefield Thornhill Street. LMA

WAKEFIELD TOWN HALL

Architectural and civic focus of the city radiating style, grace and solidity. Built between 1877 and 1880 to designs by T E Collcutt. Its sumptuous interior is the political nerve centre of Wakefield.

WAKEFIELD TRINITY WILDCATS RUGBY LEAGUE FOOTBALL CLUB

Formed in 1873 as a church side, the Wildcats have brought immense colour and vigour to the world of rugby league. Championship victors and Challenge Cup winners in 1908/09, 1945/46, 1959/60, 1961/62 and 1962/63 with a string of illustrious players such as Herbert Goodfellow, Ken Rollin and Neil Fox in their ranks, the club was involved in one of the most bizarre finals in the history of the game. Taking on Leeds at Wembley in the so-called Water Splash Final of 1968 – players aquaplaned on the paddy field surface – the team failed to miss an easy chance of victory in the dying seconds, Eddie Waring's disbelieving words: 'He's missed it! He's missed it!' haunting Don Fox who missed a conversion kick under the posts in the dying seconds. Wakefield lost 11-10. Neil Fox scored a record 6,220 points in his twenty-three year career, nineteen with Wakefield Trinity.

Wakefield Town Hall. LMA

WAKEFIELD VICARAGE

Established on Zetland Street around 1670 and occupied for the last hundred years or so by the Wakefield Conservatives, this venerable old building sits on the site of an earlier structure authorised by the Archbishop of York in 1349. Its penultimate incumbent was the ill-tempered Samuel **SHARP**. After his death in 1855, the new vicar remained in the property for twenty years, a new vicarage opening in Sandy Walk around 1875. In 1880, Edward **GREEN** bought the premises for use as a political club.

WAKEFIELD WATERFRONT

Renaissance and rejuvenation scheme which aims to restore the vitality of architecturally listed waterside buildings - Navigation Warehouses, the Rutland Mills Complex and the Phoenix Mill - for commercial, cultural, leisure and residential use. The scheme, which will incorporate the strikingly innovative **HEPWORTH GALLERY**, will act as a catalyst and focus for urban regeneration.

WAKEFIELD, WESTGATE CHAPEL
Imposing brick structure erected in 1751-52 with three-bays and pediments. Its public catacombs are the earliest such example in England, holding the coffins of some sixty local celebrities including those of textile magnates, MP's and a provincial grand master of the Freemasons.

WAKEFIELD WORKHOUSE
Workhouses originated in Elizabethan times, ideally, to offer food and shelter to displaced people in return for certain manual labours. They were generally places of degradation and were widely despised. The workhouse in Wakefield was in Thornhill Street. In 1831 it housed 103 people, the *Wakefield Journal* commenting as follows: 'In the females' day room are several idiotic and also some insane girls and, as is frequently the case, that girls of the town, full of loathsome disease, have been sent into the house, there is no separate place to put them in and they are left to mix with the other inmates whom they contaminate by their obscene language and songs.' The establishment was closed in 1852 and replaced with much improved new premises on Park Lodge Lane.

WAKEFIELD 41 INDUSTRIAL ESTATE
Industrial estate straddling the A650 portal into the city with access to junction 41 of the M1.

WAKIE OR WAKEY
Colloquial name for the county town popular with hair-gelled chavs who frequent city centre nights spots such as *Roof Tops*.

WALTON
Village famous as the home of naturalist and explorer Charles **WATERTON**. His ancestors built a hall there in 1435, the current mansion, now a modern hotel – **WALTON HALL** – replacing that structure in 1767. The original gateway of the first hall still stands. The Waterton family who lived continuously in the village from 1435 until 1876, when Edmund Waterton sold the estate, developed local coal mines and two corn mills, mining flourishing in Walton Colliery between 1890 and 1979.

WALTON HALL
Formerly the family home of Charles **WATERTON**, the eight-bayed, single-storied mansion was built on a lake island in 1767-8. Accessed by a pretty cast-iron bridge, the building was bought by Edward **SIMPSON** in 1878. It was sold again in 1940 for use as a hospital but it is now the fashionable *Walton Hall Hotel*. The grounds contain the remains of a medieval water tower and a grotto.

WARS OF THE ROSES

English Civil wars fought for dynastic supremacy between 1455 and 1485, the Lancastrians finally succumbing to the **YORKISTS** forces of Henry Tudor at Bosworth Field.

WATERTON, CHARLES

The 'Nondescript' in Wakefield Museum.
Extract from Wakefield MDC's official guide.

One of the most colourful eccentrics of the eighteenth century, Squire Waterton was a naturalist, explorer, perfecter of the art of taxidermy, an experimenter with the native poison curare, for which he was subsequently honoured by the Yorkshire Society of Anaesthetists, and a lifelong prankster. He is credited with establishing the world's first nature reserve (and devising the first ever nest box) at his **WALTON HALL** home, protected by a three miles long wall which kept poachers out and wildlife in. Completed in 1824, at a cost of £9000, the wall was funded from 'the wine I do not drink'. Born in 1782 into a distinguished Catholic family, Waterton exhibited an early fascination for adventure, visiting Spain, Barbados, Brazil, Venezuela, the United States and Canada. He famously rode on the back of a cayman and, using pioneering techniques, preserved many exotic animals and birds, some of his specimens finding their way into **WAKEFIELD MUSEUM**. He wrote a number of books including the best-selling *Wanderings in South America, the North-West of the United States and the Antilles in the Years 1812, 1816, 1820 and 1824.* He died in 1865 and is buried in the grounds of his old home. Named after him, the Waterton Lakes National Park is in Alberta, Canada. The squire was popular with local residents who were encouraged to visit his estate. He paid 6d (current equivalent of around £5) for every hedgehog brought to him unharmed for release in his grounds.

WATERTON COUNTRYSIDE EXHIBITION CENTRE

Completed in 1995, the centre rejoices in the eccentricities of Charles **WATERTON**, exhibits detailing his pioneering thoughts on wildlife and conservation. Four easy to follow trails lead from the centre around Waterton's old estate, paths accessing the lake – now known as The Heronry – the remains of the original boundary wall and Stubbs Wood where the squire often lingered. He is buried close by.

WEATHER

Wakefield district has experienced some notable weather over the centuries, the following archival snippets illustrating the extremes:

1067: After a flurry of storms, the **AIRE RIVER** flooded at **CASTLEFORD** keeping the rampaging William the Conqueror in the town for three weeks.

1714: A mighty gale blew down part of Wakefield Parish Church steeple.

Horbury, Christmas 1906. LMA

Wakefield Westgate, August Bank Holiday 1922. LMA

Flooding at Denisan's shop, Denby Dale Road.

The John Goodchild Collection. Courtesy of www.twixtaireandcalder.org.uk: The online archive of Wakefield District Images

1815: Between Wakefield and Huddersfield, a large waterspout was observed, its large black cloud resembling an inverted cone almost touching the earth. The spectacle lasted half an hour, the rain then descending in torrents.

1822: So severe were the winter storms, that the damaged Wakefield Parish Church had to be dismantled and rebuilt.

1825: On the 4th January, Wakefield was bathed in extraordinary lunar light. So effulgent was the moon, that even small print could be read without artificial illumination, many astounded residents suggesting that the glow was superior to candlelight.

Such was the mildest of the autumn in October 1825, that market gardeners harvested a second crop of strawberries in Wakefield.

On Sunday 11th January 1846 'Mrs Hirst walked to Haddlesey to see old Sally Holmes. It was so warm, she had to pull her boa off, being too hot. (From the diary of Samuel **HIRST**)

After twenty-four hours of continuous rain on November 16th 1866, the

Calder in Wakefield burst its banks ruining property valued at £50,000. There was extensive flooding in the valley of the Went. 'The view from the top of Ackworth church presented the aspect of an extensive sea dotted with islands.'

1917: On 1st April, Wakefield shivered as the thermometer plunged to minus 14 degrees centigrade.

1940: On the 28th January, 15 inches of snow fell on **PONTEFRACT**. Local bird populations were decimated.

1946/47: During one of the worst winters of the century, opencast coalmines became unworkable, the chronic shortage of gas extinguishing all street lighting, except that at main junctions, in **CASTLEFORD**.

1962: On 4th December, visibility fell to just five yards on the A1 at **FERRYBRIDGE** and **KNOTTINGLEY**, fog, described by an AA patrolman as the 'Devils Brew', making driving perilous.

1969: The meteorological party-piece known as glaze, coated the Emley Moor TV Transmitter with a jacket of ice causing it to buckle and collapse.

1965: Wakefield sweltered in a temperature of 77 degrees F on 29th March.

1976: With temperatures nudging 90 degrees F on the 25th June, heat exhaustion took its toll in Wakefield city centre. Parts of the A1 near Horbury Lagoon began to crack in the heat.

1977: Fierce winds blew swirling clouds of topsoil over the village of **WENTBRIDGE** in April, some householders having to remove six inches of dust from window ledges inside their homes.

1979: **PONTEFRACT** and **CASTLEFORD** experienced some of the worst snowfalls in living memory in January and February.

1987: On 16th October, a terrifying storm, which felled millions of trees nationwide and caused damage estimated at £1 billion, brought only minor flooding to parts of Wakefield.

1992: Thick fog caused multiple shunts on the A1 between **KNOTTINGLEY** and **WENTBRIDGE**.

'We used to be trapped in the house when the river rose in **CASTLEFORD**. You could see the floods coming down William Street. When they came, the only way you could get around the house and stay dry was to jump from one piece of furniture to the next.'

WELBECK LANDFILL

Large excavated site near **NORMANTON** between the **CALDER RIVER** and the **AIRE AND CALDER NAVIGATION** exploited over hundreds of

Wakefield Corporation dustcart, Corporation Street, Wakefield.
The John Goodchild Collection. Courtesy of www.twixtaireandcalder.org.uk: The online archive of Wakefield District Images

years for its coal, sand and gravel deposits. One of the largest landfill facilities in Europe with a final capacity of 14 million tons, the controversial site accepts domestic, commercial and toxic waste, local residents – **RATS** (Residents Against Toxic Waste Scheme) - campaigning for the raising of environmental standards.

WELSBY, JOHN

Local mining hero who worked at the West Riding Colliery. He was a member of a mines rescue team summoned to the Harmstead Pit near Birmingham after a disastrous underground fire on 4th March 1908. The rescuers battled to reach the twenty-six trapped men but they had all succumbed to the heat and flames. Welsby also died. He was buried after an emotional funeral at **ALTOFTS** Parish Church on 14th March 1908, thousands of mourners attending his funeral.

The old Bay Horse and bridge. LMA

ROBIN HOOD - WENTBRIDGE.
One of the only place names that can be located in 'A Lytell Geste of Robyn Hode' (c.1492-1534) is the Sayles now known as Brockadale, Wentbridge.
'And walke up to Saylis,
And so to Watlinge Stret (e).
And Wayte after some unkuth gest,
Up Chance ye may them mete.'

Plaque at Wentbridge remembering Robin Hood. LMA

WENTBRIDGE

Village on the line of the **GREAT NORTH ROAD** its viaduct spanning the deeply incised valley of the River Went. The decorative village bridge bears a plaque to the local exploits of Robin **HOOD**. The steep and heavily wooded valley, on the main coaching route between London and Scotland, was ideal for ambush and many highwaymen and vagabonds including William **NEVISON** operated in the area. Two local inns, *The Gate* and the **BLUE BELL INN**, became notorious. Nearby, is the picturesque church of St John built in 1878.

WENT RIVER

Nineteen-mile long stream rising from a spring in **FEATHERSTONE** and flowing generally east through **WENTBRIDGE** to the confluence with the Don north of Thorne. Its name means clear, pure and bright. Watering the lovely Broc-o-dale ('the haunt of badgers') it once attracted witches including the notorious Mary **PANNEL**. The outlaw Robin **HOOD** frequented its banks. The road through its precipitous valley in **WENTBRIDGE**, was regarded by stagecoach operators as the most taxing between London and Edinburgh.

John Wesley. LMA

WESLEY, JOHN

This capable preacher and founder of Methodism gave early support to the establishment of the denomination in Wakefield. He toured tirelessly throughout the district and opened Wakefield's first purpose-built Methodist Chapel in Thornhill Street in 1774. By the time of the evangelist's death in 1791, he is estimated to have preached an astonishing 40,000 sermons to millions of followers and to have travelled some 300,000 miles. The movement broke away from the established Church of England in 1795.

WESTFIELD RESOURCE AND ENTERPRISE CENTRE

Community facility established in **SOUTH ELMSALL** - an area adversely affected by pit closures – offering business advice, adult education, an NUM health advisory centre and conference facilities.

WESTGATE RUN

Celebrated Wakefield Westgate pub-crawl taking in twenty-two licensed premises starting at the **REDOUBT** and ending at the **BLACK ROCK**. Young people from all over the north of England converge on Wakefield at weekends, the run, which is often attempted for charity, particularly attracting hen and stag parties.

WEST RIDING

Centred on the administrative capital of Wakefield, one of the three ancient divisions of the county of Yorkshire covering some 1,766,664 acres. The term 'riding' is derived from the word 'thridding' meaning a third part.

WEST RIDING PAUPER LUNATIC ASYLUM

Mental institution opened for the 'insane poor' on a site near **STANLEY** in 1818. The H-shaped facility cost £36,000 to build and was designed to accommodate 150 patients, the population rising to 1469 inmates by 1900. Following intervention by its first two pioneering medical directors, Doctor Ellis and Charles Caesar **CORSELLIS**, the regime at the asylum was regarded as enlightened, facilities including a church and a theatre added in 1859. Inmates were encouraged to read and write and to participate in meaningful work such as baking, weaving and boot mending, the less active among them being regularly exercised in grassed yards known as 'airing courts'. Food was plentiful and wholesome consisting of bread, milk, yeast dumplings, meat, potatoes and beer but some original treatments were primitive and barbaric. The 'revolving chair' – patients were strapped in and spun round at over 100 revolutions per minute – was particularly feared and detested, the practice ending in 1821. Records identify a number of bizarre diagnoses, inmates being committed for eccentricities such as 'political excitement' and reading plays and novels! The facility eventually became **STANLEY ROYD HOSPITAL**.

WEST RIDING REGISTRY OF DEEDS

In 1701, local justices petitioned Parliament pointing out that: '...the West Riding of the County of Yorkshire is the principal place in the North for cloth manufacture, and most of the traders therein are freeholders, and have frequent occasions to borrow money, but for want of a Register find it difficult to give security to the satisfaction of the money lender, by the means thereof the said trade is very much obstructed and many families ruined.' This initial petition failed, but the justices persevered and, at the third attempt, their wishes were granted. Only the second such registry in England was founded and opened in 1704 on a site opposite **WAKEFIELD CATHEDRAL** (now occupied by Marks and Spencer). The registry moved to its current site on Newstead Road, Wakefield in 1932 becoming the West Yorkshire Archive Service. The registry safeguards local authority, public body and ecclesiastical records and also has extensive archive material relating to local businesses, industries, schools, trades unions, sports clubs and political organisations.

WEST YORKSHIRE ASTRONOMICAL SOCIETY
Founded in 1973 in the grounds of Carleton Community Centre in **PONTEFRACT**, the society is a registered charity, its members constructing the **ROSSE OBSERVATORY**.

WEST YORKSHIRE POLICE
Regional headquarters of the county constabulary situated in Laburnum Road, Wakefield.

WHITWOOD COLLIERY
The Whitwood area of **CASTLEFORD** was dominated by the colliery owned by Henry **BRIGGS**. The pit closed after ninety-five years of production in 1968.

WHITWOOD MERE INFANTS SCHOOL
Designed by ground-breaking architect Oliver Hill, the school was built in 1939-40 in the pure Modernist style. The building, which is today regarded as a historical monument, is curvilinear in shape, its orientation and generous fenestration ensuring the optimum exploitation of sunlight. Externally the fabric is decorated with an attractive faience tiled frieze.

WIFE MURDER
In December 1880, colliery worker Thomas Beckett killed his cheating twenty-nine-year-old wife Hannah at their hovel in Old Soaphouse Yard in Walton. Driven to despair by his spouse's adultery, he confronted her, the pair bizarrely agreeing to kill each other. Hannah took up a knife and stabbed her husband. He, in turn, slashed his wife's throat with a razor. Some time later, the heavily bleeding couple were found intertwined on top of their bed. Hannah was dead but Thomas survived and was later charged with murder. Thomas faced justice at the Leeds Assizes in February 1881, his lawyer speaking with great persuasion and eloquence of incredible forbearance,

toleration and provocation. He asked for clemency. The sympathetic judge guided the jury to consider a verdict of manslaughter and Beckett was convicted of the lesser crime, the judge sentencing him to just four days in prison. After hearing the sentence, the hard-of-hearing Beckett swooned thinking he had been committed to prison for fourteen years. His fears were soon allayed and he was released, having already served the allotted time in gaol.

WIFE SALES
Celebrated throughout Yorkshire for their good husbandry, Wakefield residents were pioneers in the socially aware practice of recycling. In 1815, a man sold his wife in a **PONTEFRACT** Market Place auction. She was offered at a minimum price of one shilling but her spouse gleefully 'knocked her down' for eleven shillings. Earlier still in 1776, Mr John Nutt delivered his wife in a halter to **PONTEFRACT BUTTERCROSS** and sold her to a Mr Ryder for just five shillings, commenting: 'All persons seemed perfectly satisfied'.

WINN FAMILY
The Winn's have owned the **NOSTELL PRIORY** estate since the middle of the seventeenth century. The founder of the dynasty is said to been a draper to Elizabeth I who granted the family arms in 1604. A subsequent opportunist married a rich London merchant's daughter and invested his wealth in Yorkshire. The head of the family today is Lord St Oswald.

WINTERSETT RESERVOIR
Built in 1854 (the adjacent Cold Hiendley followed in 1874) to address water shortage problems in the **BARNSLEY CANAL**. A redundant Cornish tin mine beam engine was installed to pump water in 1875. The reservoir has long been used for recreation. In hard winters, one **RYHILL** man set up a small stove and sold hot pies and peas to skaters. Today, the reservoir forms part of the **HERONRY AND WATERTON COUNTRYSIDE DISCOVERY CENTRE**.

WOLFENDEN, LORD JOHN FREDERICK
A former pupil of **WAKEFIELD QUEEN ELIZABETH'S GRAMMAR SCHOOL**, (he later married the daughter of one of its former headmasters) Wolfenden became a philosophy tutor at Oxford, the headmaster of Uppingham School and the vice-chancellor of Reading University. An outstanding administrator and committee chairman, he was commissioned to examine the law relating to homosexuality, producing his influential report in 1957. He had an openly gay son whose tragic death is recounted in *The Fatal Attraction* by Sebastian Faulk. Wolfenden was awarded the OBE in 1942. He received a knighthood in 1956 and a life peerage in 1974.

WOOD STREET, WAKEFIELD

The forum and civic heart of the city, its array of heroic and sumptuously classical buildings including **WAKEFIELD COUNTY HALL,** Wakefield Court House, **WAKEFIELD TOWN HALL** and **WAKEFIELD MUSEUM.**

WOOLLEY

On the still somewhat remote southern periphery of the district, the 'wolves shelter' has been an important settlement since ancient times, the antecedents of many notable families such as the Wentworths having connections with Monk Bretton Priory and **PONTEFRACT CASTLE**. Much of the present Woolley Hall dates from 1772. Its grounds were once enclosed as a hunting park in the reign of Henry VII. St Peter's Church – the bosses and heraldic shields shed light on the lineage of important local families – is one of Wakefield's most interesting. The plague reached the village in 1666, local magistrates instructing that constables be stationed at the doors of infected houses to prevent entry and contamination. In a postscript to their decree, they ordered: 'And you are to take care that ye effect and purport of this Warrant be as fully and duly executed upon the family or persons belonging to ye Hall or house of Mr. Wentworth as any other.'

WOOLLEY EDGE

Escarpment overlooking the M1 Motorway with magnificent views towards Emley Moor. A locally discovered flint axe shows that ancient man settled here around 6000 years ago, unearthed flints and scrapers also attesting to Iron Age occupation around the start of the first millennium.

WORLD COAL CARRYING CHAMPIONSHIPS

Annual athletic events founded by Fred HIRST, held every Easter Monday in the village of **GAWTHORPE** on the outskirts of **OSSETT**, thirty competitors carrying one hundredweight (50 kilogram) sacks of coal over a coarse measuring 1012 metres starting at the *Royal Oak* and ending at the maypole on the village green. The event has its origins in backslap and 'backslavver', a customer entering the pub in 1963 and cheekily tapping a chum on the shoulder with the words: 'Ba gum lad, tha' looks buggered!' The pal retorted: 'Ah'm as fit as thee an if tha' dun't believe me, gerra bagga coil on thi' back and 'ah'll get one on mine and 'ah'll race thee to t'top o't'wood!' And so was born an unlikely contest that has been held every year since, the fairer sex competing in their own race carrying smaller 20 kilogram bags. The world records stand at 4 minutes 6 seconds for the men's race and 5 minutes 5 seconds for the ladies race.

WRAGBY BAR
Part of the original bar toll-house on the former Redhouse and Crofton **TURNPIKE ROAD** survives on the highway just outside **NOSTELL**. Tolls were once levied according to the number of horses and the types of vehicles that sought to use the privately constructed highways.

WRENTHORPE
Originally named Potovens (locally 'Potoil') in allusion to the local pottery industry which was one of the earliest recorded in northern England, the village was important during the nineteenth century for market gardening, forced **RHUBARB** being a speciality. Rope and twine manufacturing, the production of woollen goods and railway shunting and marshalling of coal wagons in the extensive marshalling yards around Wrenthorpe Junction, brought significant employment during the mining era. Wrenthorpe Mission once gained notoriety as the site of a miracle. A crippled miner with a back injury was visited by two pastors who anointed him with sewing machine oil! The man walked, causing scores of locals to leave their pubs in astonishment. The village is home to **SILCOATES SCHOOL**.

WROE'S MANSION
Built between 1856 and 1857 by John Wroe, the self-styled 'Yorkshire Moses' on the corner of Brandy Carr Lane, the stone house was paid for from subscriptions, the dubious prophet persuading followers of his Christian Israelite sect to donate at least ten percent of their earnings to the fund. At one time, fund receipts exceeded the trade income for the entire town! Wroe promised his followers that they would never die. He perished in 1862.

XSCAPE
Lifestyle entertainment and sporting centre at Junction 32 of the M62 Motorway offering a multiplex cinema and bowling alley and indoor facilities for climbing and skiing on real ice and snow. It is part of the **GLASSHOUGHTON BUSINESS, LEISURE AND RETAIL PARK**.

YELLOLY, ROBERT
Chief Constable of Wakefield between 1920 and 1942. He was noted as a strict disciplinarian and for insisting that recruits come from outside the area.

His tenure was marked by increased mobility and improvements in communications. He was awarded the MBE in March 1920 for his war service. He famously once instructed that all vehicles observed by his constables between the hours of midnight and six in the morning should have their descriptions, registrations and directions of travel recorded as a measure against rising crime.

YORKISTS
During the **WARS OF THE ROSES**, supporters of the House of York whose emblem was and still is the white rose. Legend has it that after the Yorkists' pivotal victory at the Battle of Towton in 1461, the local roses forever bloomed with sanguinary blushes of red on their petals. The cricketer Lord Martin Bladen **HAWKE** used the white rose as a motif for his Yorkshire club.

YORKSHIRE ART CIRCUS
Community arts and publishing organisation based in Glasshoughton, **CASTLEFORD** specialising in creative writing – especially for first-time writers – IT and publishing.

YORKSHIRE DAY
Inaugurated by the Yorkshire Ridings Society, the 1 August celebrations commemorate the Battle of Minden fought on that day in 1759 between the Anglo-Allied army under the command of Ferdinand of Brunswick and the French. Despite the British victory, many Yorkshire soldiers died in the action but some of their surviving comrades picked souvenir white roses from the field. This action may have inspired the Yorkshire emblem.

YORKSHIRE MOTTO
Recipe for life eagerly embraced by all Wakefield residents: 'Hear all, see all and say nowt, eat all, sup all and pay nowt and if tha ever does owt for nowt, do it for thissen.' When questions about second helpings were ventured at meal times, even well upholstered miners would thrust out their plates and respond: 'Yus please. T'belly keeps t'back up. You can't work without some packing.'

YORKSHIRE PENNIES (see PONTEFRACT CAKE)

YORKSHIRE SCULPTURE PARK
International centre for modern and contemporary

Typical Wakefield Tyke. LMA

sculpture set in 500 acres of parkland and gardens, originally the private grounds of **BRETTON HALL**. Exhibits include works by Barbara **HEPWORTH**, Anthony Caro, Antony Gormley, Elizabeth Frink and Sol LeWitt, bronze pieces by Henry **MOORE** forming one of the largest open-air displays of his work anywhere in the world.

A modern version of a Minotaur, Yorkshire Sculpture Park. LMA

Z

ZIVILINTERNIERUNGLASGER

Internment camp for Germans, Austrians and Turks who were present in Britain at the outbreak of the First World War. The camp was established at a commandeered **LOFTHOUSE PARK**, interment affecting all visiting aliens and even foreigners resident or working in the UK. Prisoners included dozens of eminent professors, scores of intellectuals and lecturers and two German butchers from Wakefield! The camp initially housed 1500 internees, the later imprisonment of combatants raising the number to 2400. Life at the camp was civilised and relaxed, prisoners growing their own food, developing a 600 book library, playing games and organising a series of business and commercial courses.

ZOUCH, HENRY

Born at **SANDAL MAGNA** in 1724, Zouch became minister at the village church. He died in 1795, directing, in his will, that he should be buried in the garden of Sandal Hall on the south-western side of the churchyard, having always maintained that this land was within the church glebe. The owner of the hall refused to comply with the wishes of the deceased but the executors of the will were determined to follow the instructions. Accordingly, they buried the old boy as near to the disputed boundary wall as possible, digging a trench under the wall and pushing the coffin into the hall garden!